COACHING
COPYRIGHT

ALA Editions purchases fund advocacy, awareness,
and accreditation programs for library professionals worldwide.

COACHING COPYRIGHT

Edited by
KEVIN L. SMITH
and
ERIN L. ELLIS

ALA
Editions

CHICAGO   2020

Extensive effort has gone into ensuring the reliability of the information in this book; however, the publisher makes no warranty, express or implied, with respect to the material contained herein.

ISBNs
978-0-8389-1848-7 (paper)
978-0-8389-1881-4 (PDF)
978-0-8389-1879-1 (ePub)
978-0-8389-1880-7 (Kindle)

Library of Congress Cataloging-in-Publication Data

Names: Smith, Kevin L. (Kevin Lindsay), 1959- editor. | Ellis, Erin L., editor.
Title: Coaching copyright / edited by Kevin L. Smith and Erin L. Ellis.
Description: Chicago : ALA Editions, 2020. | Includes bibliographical references and index.
Identifiers: LCCN 2018055616 | ISBN 9780838918487 (print : alk. paper) | ISBN
    9780838918791 (epub : alk. paper) | ISBN 9780838918807 (kindle : alk. paper) |
    ISBN 9780838918814 (pdf : alk. paper)
Subjects: LCSH: Copyright—United States. | Library copyright policies—United States. |
    Library orientation—United States. | Librarians—United States—Handbooks,
    manuals, etc.
Classification: LCC KF2995 .C576 2019 | DDC 346.7304/82—dc23
LC record available at https://lccn.loc.gov/2018055616

Cover design by Karen Sheets de Gracia.

Text design in the Chaparral, Gotham, and Bell Gothic typefaces.

♾ This paper meets the requirements of ANSI/NISO Z39.48-1992 (Permanence of Paper).

Printed in the United States of America

24 23 22 21 20   5 4 3 2 1

Contents

Preface

WHEN THE IDEA OF A BOOK TITLED "COACHING COPYRIGHT" was first suggested to us, we were skeptical about the title. But as we thought about it, we realized that coaching, whether one thinks of athletic coaching or the use of the word in corporate or professional contexts, was very appropriate to the situation we were being asked to address. Coaching requires a very practical approach to solving problems in specific and definable situations. Copyright education, too, is best when placed within a specific context. When librarians are asked to assist with copyright questions that arise in an educational context, coaching is exactly the approach they need to take.

This book, then, is intended to provide a practical guide for the person called upon to serve as a "copyright librarian," or, indeed, anyone who is confronted with copyright dilemmas. Rather than focusing on an abstract explication of copyright law, it focuses on coaching as a framework for addressing specific copyright problems and issues, and on techniques for teaching about copyright to various audiences.

The structure of the book is dictated by this approach. The first part of the book consists of two chapters that provide general overviews of the topic of copyright coaching. The first chapter examines what it means to be a copyright coach, explicates a framework that such a coach can follow when confronted with a specific issue, and lays out the legal and practical considerations, in a condensed way, that need to be considered at each step of that framework.

In the second chapter, Jill Becker and Erin Ellis place the idea of coaching in general, and coaching copyright in particular, firmly in the context of library instruction, as well as in the ACRL's "Framework for Information Literacy in Higher Education." They discuss coaching as a high-impact practice that positions learners in an ideal space for understanding the nuances of copyright.

The second and longer part of this book continues the emphasis on practical applications, with eight case studies written by specialists in library instruction and in copyright. Laura Quilter's initial chapter is a catalog of helpful techniques for "hooking your audience on copyright," and this is followed by two chapters on specific techniques that can help convey important copyright topics: Anne Gilliland describes storytelling as an effective method, and Ana Enriquez describes role-playing as a successful approach. The next four case studies address specific audiences and contexts. Merinda Kaye Hensley focuses on opportunities to work with undergraduate research journals, and Anali Perry discusses her efforts in working with instructional designers. The next two chapters demonstrate approaches to helping administrators come to terms with copyright on campus: Stephanie Davis-Kahl and Karen Schmidt write about a liberal arts college context, and Carla Myers writes about the university context. The book closes with a report by Will Cross on a research study conducted to assess the effectiveness of an LIS class on legal issues, which includes assessments of specific instructional techniques, as well as a brief glimpse of what the future of coaching about copyright and other legal issues for librarians might look like.

KEVIN L. SMITH

1

Coaching Copyright

Rules and Strategies for the Game

BEING A COPYRIGHT COACH

Recently, a former colleague of my wife's, a clinician at a major U.S. hospital, got in touch with me to ask a question about a diagnostic manual he had written. He was not primarily a researcher, so he was unsure about how he should deal with copyright, licensing, and publication for the manual that his hospital superiors were encouraging him to distribute. Like so many academics, he was especially concerned about attribution—he wanted to receive proper credit for his work—and he was worried that less experienced practitioners might make changes detrimental to the value of his manual. He had heard of the Creative Commons (CC) licenses and thought such a license might work for him, but he needed help to understand the CC licensing scheme and figure out how to apply one to his own work.

This situation is a nice example of "coaching" copyright. As a professor who teaches copyright in a law school, I strive for my students to gain a complete and detailed understanding of copyright law and the issues involved, and I try to proceed in a systematic way. But my position with this clinician was quite different. He did not want a comprehensive lesson in copyright law. In fact, such a lesson would not help; it would likely confuse him and still leave him unsure about how to proceed. What my friend needed was coaching—a practical path forward that would help him achieve a specific goal. Coaching is distinguished from teaching because it is focused on a particular client's need and on obtaining a desired outcome for that client.

The clinician and I began our consultation through e-mail, and I used this initial exchange to establish some basic parameters: details about the manual in question, the kind of distribution he had in mind, and what misuse(s) he was concerned with preventing. With these basic parameters established, we sat down for a more detailed discussion. I had determined that there should be three stages to our discussion.

First, we needed to be sure that my friend was, in fact, the copyright holder in this manual. We needed to discuss the possibility that it could be considered a work made for hire and therefore owned by his employer, the hospital. I began to ask some questions about the relationship of the manual to his work, and he quickly understood that work for hire was a likely conclusion. We then discussed what further information he needed to gather to make a determination about ownership; primarily, what the hospital's intellectual property (IP) policy could tell us.

Our second area of discussion was, as I indicated above, what precise uses he had in mind for the manual. Was the distribution to be limited to a group of colleagues, or did he plan a general publication on the Internet? Did he envision some kind of academic publication in the future? What were the things he was worried about, that is, the things he wanted to use a license to protect against? Here I tried to explain how the CC provisions work, and made suggestions about which would best meet his needs. Since the initial distribution of the manual was to be quite limited, and later publication was planned, we agreed that a fairly restrictive license—author attribution, noncommercial, no derivative works—would best preserve his options for whatever next steps he might consider.

Finally, we settled on a series of steps he should take:

1. He should determine whether he or the hospital was the rights holder through examination of the hospital's IP policy and discussion with his supervisor.
2. He should register the work with the Copyright Office. I explained, only in general terms, that registration carries some advantages he might want to preserve. I also knew that some form of registration was important to him, since he had come into our conversation believing that Creative Commons offered a kind of registry that would help protect him. I explained that this was not the case, but that registration was both possible, through the Copyright Office, and advisable.
3. We discussed the practical details about how he could apply a CC license to his work, even while it was just being distributed in print

format, and how he could use the icon and code provided by CC later if he posted his manual to the Internet.

4. Finally, we talked about possible publication outlets for the manual, or an article about it, and how the steps we had developed would help preserve his options when he came to that point.

It is important to note that throughout this encounter, I wanted to gather enough information to point my friend in the direction he wanted to go. I am a strong supporter of Creative Commons and open licensing, but I did not immediately embrace his suggestion of a CC license and give a lecture about the benefits of the CC-BY license. Had I done so, I probably would have been ignored, and the encounter would have been unproductive, both for me, and more importantly, for my client. The focus had to remain on his needs and desired outcomes in order for this to be a successful coaching session.

There are two further observations I want to make, based on this short case study.

First, I want to comment on using the word *client* to refer to those who inquire about copyright issues with librarians. In general, librarians do not think of library patrons as their clients, but I suggest there are good reasons to do so, especially in the context of coaching copyright. As someone who has studied to qualify for three different professions (law, the clergy, and librarianship), I have given a lot of thought to what makes an occupation a profession. The distinguished legal scholar Roscoe Pound famously defined a profession as "a group of men [*sic*] pursuing a learned art as a common calling in the spirit of public service."[1] Putting aside the grossly outdated assumption that only men could be part of a profession (it was incorrect even when Pound made it), the three elements of this definition—learning, organization, and public service, are all extremely important. However, there is another element that helps define professions—in almost all cases, a professional is someone who pursues public service by applying specialized learning *to the particular situations of individuals*. Professionals work one client at a time. Rather like a coach trying to adjust to a specific game situation, a professional's thought process is to analyze, diagnose, and then advise about the unique and individual situation presented by a particular client. This aspect of professionalism is shared by both lawyers and librarians, and it is a useful reminder that whenever a library patron presents a copyright question to a librarian, her response should be calibrated to the details of the unique situation and the outcomes that the patron, or client, if you will, is seeking.

Therefore, I will refer throughout this chapter to *clients*, because this word reminds us that we must approach copyright education in libraries one person, and one unique set of issues, problems, and needs, at a time. That word also calls to mind the high standard of professionalism that is required of us, as librarians, especially when we are called upon to discuss legal questions and ramifications with a patron.

This leads to another point I should make about the story with which I began this chapter. There is an important difference between how I approach a copyright question and how most librarians should proceed. I am a lawyer, and I hold licenses to practice law in two states, although both are now inactive. The result is that I have more leeway to cross the line between information and legal advice when I talk with a client. I still have to be careful that the client understands the nature of our relationship, perhaps with *more* care precisely because, as a lawyer, I need to be very attentive to if, and when, a lawyer/client relationship is established. While librarians do not face this issue, it is still vital that our clients understand that we can offer information, and even discuss options based on the information we uncover, but we cannot advise about specific courses of action, nor can we offer our clients opinions about liability or the legal advisability of their choices.[2]

Librarians are frequently called upon to teach patrons about copyright. Sometimes that involves classroom sessions, often as part of a larger program of library instruction, during which basic information about the copyright law is imparted. Coaching is distinguished from this kind of teaching by its focus on an individual's specific situation. But coaching, like librarianship in general, is also distinguished from giving legal advice because, in the large majority of cases, the coach is not able to give such advice. The coach's role is focused on helping the client understand their particular situation and, based on information the coach can impart, determine a course of action that will help the individual achieve their goals. Essentially, the librarian as copyright advisor is in the same position as other subject specialists in a library; the subject specialization just happens to be copyright—and as such, provides information to clients on the same terms.

One of the best reasons for using the analogy with coaching is that to coach is to focus on strategy and risk management. Likewise, when librarians discuss copyright situations with clients, they should focus on strategy and risk management. The information that librarians can supply is best applied when it is used to figure out which of the available options are most likely to accomplish the client's goals while reducing the risk of accusations of copyright infringement. Risk, however, is a two-edged sword. When discussing risk with a client, it is important to help them assess the risk inherent in *not* pursuing their goal. These lost "opportunity costs" are very real; what is lost, for example, if a collection that could be valuable to scholars is not digitized because of fear that a few items may pose the risk of someone objecting to their inclusion? Are there ways to come to terms with that risk which do not undermine the entire project? It is only within the context of this kind of comprehensive assessment of risk, from a multitude of perspectives, that we can help clients make decisions.

KEEPING IT SIMPLE

When our clients come to us with a copyright question, they are seeking answers that are clear, understandable, and easy to put into practice. Often, they want a "yes or no" answer. In short, they want us to keep it simple. But the copyright law in the United States is not simple at all. The book published by the Library of Congress, *Copyright Law of the United States, and Related Laws Contained in Title 17 of the United States Code*, runs to over 350 pages. As this title implies, the application of the copyright law is further complicated by its interrelationship with other laws, as well as international treaties. And, like many other laws, Title 17 of the U.S. Code is structured in ways that make it unintuitive. Most, but not all, definitions are grouped in one place (section 101), while some key terms are not defined at all.[3] Exceptions abound, and one must often read the entire provision of the law, plus other portions to which a provision might refer, in order to piece together an answer to a copyright question. Also, the language used throughout the code, while common in legislation, seems convoluted to most people (even many lawyers!) and difficult to map onto specific issues or situations. Finally, the situation grows and evolves through case law, which means that different contexts, circumstances, and judicial philosophies play a significant role in fully comprehending the state of the law. So how can we hope to deliver a clear and usable answer to a client who is faced with a specific situation she must address? I suggest three important techniques.

First, it is important to focus on the specific situation that concerns the client. Sometimes you will have to broaden the issue, or introduce concerns that the client has not thought of—like the ownership issue I raised with the clinician in my opening example. But a copyright consultation is still about a particular set of circumstances, and it should not be used as an opportunity to try to teach the client everything you know about copyright, or to discuss the fascinating, but unrelated, case that you just read. You should focus on what the client needs to know to make a decision, clearly explain the relevant legal concepts, discuss the options for their specific application, and restrain the urge to go off on tangents.

An analogy with coaching a sport is again useful here. For example, there is a clear difference between those times when a basketball coach is teaching her players different aspects of the game in the gym, and what is done during the game. Like young athletes, the game is moving very fast for our clients; they are caught up in a swirl of different ideas, advice, and anxieties. And like the coach during the game, we need to offer targeted, specific, and clear information—how should I defend against the next shot, who should I look for when bringing the ball down the court? These are not times for a lesson on the proper form for shooting foul shots; the need is for situationally appropriate instructions that are clear and focus on the specific dilemma at hand. You may, and in fact, should, find opportunities to teach more expansively about copyright, but for the particular client who has a problem, it is important to focus on that problem and its solution.

WHY LAWYERS SAY "IT DEPENDS," AND WHY YOU SHOULD TOO

Clients are frequently bemused, and often downright angry, when a lawyer says "it depends" in answer to a question. This reply is, allegedly, so ubiquitous that there are a good many lawyer jokes predicated on it. But I want to defend "it depends" for a moment, because it is an important counterbalance to my advice to keep things as simple as possible.

In most situations, when someone who is asked for legal advice or information says "it depends," the phrase means one of two things.

First, it can often signal that the advisor simply does not yet have enough information to offer a firm answer. This situation arises because so many copyright questions are extremely dependent on specific facts and circumstances. Another common legal aphorism is "change the facts, change the answer." There is almost no copyright question or conundrum where the advisor is given all the necessary facts at the start, and there are even fewer all-purpose answers that do not depend on the circumstantial background. This is a familiar situation for librarians, of course, since we are trained in reference interview techniques, where we have to elicit the context for the question as asked before we can answer the question as really needed. People seldom directly ask exactly what they need to know, and likewise, they rarely, if ever, provide all the important information when they describe a copyright conundrum. So the advisor must probe more deeply, often asking questions around the edges of the situation because what the client thought was relevant to an answer may be quite different from the facts that are actually needed. This is also partly a result of the law being so unintuitive.

The other thing an advisor often means when she tells a client that "it depends" is that the ultimate answer depends on the client herself—her goals, values, and tolerance for risk. A non-attorney librarian, of course, should never tell a client that the answer to his question is precisely this, or his course of action is exactly that. The truth is, however, that lawyers often cannot do that either, because the ultimate decision belongs to the client. The client must decide how important it is to do what they are seeking to do, in the context of the potential risks that have been explained to them. The client knows what she is trying to accomplish, what the institutional mission is, and how central the specific activity might be to that goal or mission. The client, and only the client, can balance the risk equation in a way that is comfortable (or, at least, less uncomfortable).

There are several reasons why a librarian should not answer a copyright question with direct advice. Avoiding the unauthorized practice of law is one. Another is respect for the general role of the librarian in all information-seeking situations, which is to provide that information from authoritative sources, not to suggest answers simply because they seem right to the individual librarian. An important additional reason is that in most situations involving copyright, the context of the decision is personal to the client, so the librarian, and even a lawyer, must respect the boundaries of the relationship.

EXAMPLES AND ANALOGIES

One of the steepest obstacles when helping people understand and use copyright to resolve dilemmas is the gap that many people experience between the rules and the application of those rules. I have often had the experience of walking someone through the applicable principles of copyright, and seeing all the indications that they have understood, only to discover that the last step—the way to apply those principles to their situation—is still beyond them. I have come to believe that the problem here is a lack of examples. There is a sound reason why law students are taught by reading cases. Using the case method, which was first introduced at the Harvard Law School in the 1870s by then-Dean Christopher Columbus Langdell, forces students to extract the rule or principle from the circumstances of a particular situation.[4] The gap I am describing is thus avoided; there is no point where the rule has to be applied, because the rule has emerged, for the student, from its application. This method has been so enduring in law schools, I believe, because it helps new lawyers get comfortable handling patterns of fact, and trains them in application of the law to those facts from their very first day.

It is impractical, of course, to import the case method of teaching law into copyright coaching situations; as I have said, clients in those consultations are seeking practical, understandable direction and do not want extensive lessons on the history and development of the law. But I believe there are two reasons to keep the case method very much in mind during copyright coaching.

First, reading cases is a fantastic way for a coach to improve her knowledge and skills. Just as athletic coaches watch game films, reading cases helps the copyright coach develop a nuanced grasp of how specific facts are analyzed under various provisions of the law, and it provides a store of examples to share with clients. And that is the second reason why a copyright coach should know the case law; because analogies with similar situations that have arisen and been decided in the past help clients grasp the contours of their own position. One does not have to go into great detail about a particular case, but when the coach understands how previous decisions have been made, she can say things like, "There was an important case where the reduced size and definition of images was treated as favorable under the third factor in a fair use analysis.[5] That consideration also would support your fair use position."

There is really no substitute for familiarity with case law. Learning "black letter" copyright law—that is, the body of well-established copyright laws that are no longer in reasonable dispute—is important for the copyright coach, but it is not sufficient. In many areas, there simply is no black letter rule that will resolve an issue. And, as I've said, black letter rules often confuse clients, even if they understand them, because they can't see how to apply them to their situations. Knowing about cases, and applying that knowledge sparingly and in a targeted way, is the key to successful copyright coaching.

SPOTTING THE ISSUES

Issue-spotting is another skill that is heavily stressed for law students; it involves identifying which issues really need to be resolved in order for a client to move forward, as well as recognizing which issues are distractions. Our clients often stumble over the task of issue-spotting, focusing on the distractions and missing the real problems. Indeed, copyright advisors also struggle with this; it simply is a challenging task that requires a careful and methodical approach.

Over the years, I have found that one approach to copyright issue-spotting is to work through five separate questions, in a specific order. Taken in order, these questions help to identify where the problem and the potential resolution lie.[6] Is the question whether or not a work has risen into the public domain, or is it whether a particular use of that work might be fair use? Should we focus on the application of the face-to-face teaching exception, or is our energy best spent finding the rights holder in order to ask permission? We don't naturally pose these kinds of questions to ourselves, but confusions like these can stymie efforts to help a client accomplish her goals. To clarify any copyright situation, then, an advisor can work through the following five questions, in the order presented:

1. Is there a copyright?
2. Is there a license that helps determine this issue?
3. Does a specific exception in the copyright law apply?
4. Is this a fair use?
5. Who should I ask for permission?

If the determination on the first question is that the work involved does not have a copyright, then it is not necessary to apply the remaining questions. If there is a specific exception that will authorize the desired activity, a fair use analysis may be unnecessary. And if none of the first four questions resolve the question, seeking permission may be the best remaining alternative.

Often clients will come to us focused on one issue, and our role is to redirect their energies. They may focus, for example, on finding a rights holder from whom to ask permission, when permission may be unnecessary because the use is clearly fair use. Thinking about these questions, and working through them in order, will often help the advisor recognize the need for information that a client does not realize is relevant, and provide an opportunity to elicit that information.

We will use these five questions to organize the remainder of this chapter. It is important to note that while these questions provide a useful framework for analyzing any copyright issue, none of them are actually easy questions, and there are many possible facets to each one. We will try to unpack those facets in what follows, and will be sure to approach each of them in a way that addresses situations in which a client is concerned about protecting or sharing her own work, as well as situations where the work of someone else is being used.

THE RULES OF THE GAME
Examining Our Five Questions

As we turn to examine each of these five questions in turn, it is helpful to begin our consideration of the first question—Does the work in question have a copyright that must be considered?—from the perspective of the client who is interested in protecting her own work. The issue of whether or not a copyright exists often comes to us from someone who has created a new work, and wants to know how to "get" a copyright for it. This is an excellent opportunity to talk with the client about the proper subject matter for copyright, automatic protection, work made for hire, and the advantages of copyright registration and notice.

Automatic protection, of course, is the most fundamental issue about obtaining copyright that many of our clients do not understand. There is a long history in the United States of requiring "formalities" in order to obtain protection, so it is not surprising that, even decades after the United States did away with the last of its formalities,[7] people still believe that some affirmative action is needed to protect a work with copyright. The idea that protection is automatic, that copyright "subsists . . . in original works of authorship" immediately when they are "fixed in any tangible medium of protection,"[8] ought to be a comfort to worried clients, but in my experience it often is not. Creators simply worry about whether their copyright is real if they don't "do something" about it. So it is very important to reassure clients that they *do* have protection, and have had it since the moment of creation, but it can also help to tell them that there are advantages to taking some affirmative actions related to that protection.

The most basic action a creator can take to enforce the copyright protection that he holds is to provide notice of their rights so that potential users will know immediately that the work is protected and will also know who to contact for permission to use the work. Copyright coaches should work with all creators to figure out the best form of notice to provide based on the medium of the work, but there should be very few situations where notice is impossible or undesirable. A Creative Commons license, about which we shall say more later, is an excellent form of notice, as is (if appropriate) the more traditional "All rights reserved, Kevin L. Smith, 2018." Notice is a direct communication between the creator and users, and it can take many different forms. Creators can be creative in thinking about what rights they want to reserve and which they should share, but some form of notice about who they are, what they want for their work, and how to contact them is key to using copyright in a balanced way.

Registration has several advantages, and for many creators it can provide peace of mind as well. Since registration is inexpensive and easy—it can be done online,[9] and the basic fee is between $35 and $55—it is a simple way to address a particular question that many creators have: "If copyright is automatic, how can I prove that I was the actual creator of this work?" Registration provides prima facie evidence of copyright ownership, so suggesting prompt registration to a nervous creator can help quite a bit in this situation and is much more effective than the old rumor that one should send the work to oneself through registered mail. There are other advantages to registration as well. Registration is necessary to file an infringement claim in federal court, and if it is done in a timely way,[10] it also entitles the rights holder to ask for statutory damages if their work is infringed. Thus, while it is important to help a creator understand that registration is not required and protection exists whether or not the work is registered, there will be a lot of situations where advising the client to register her work will make good sense.

Both with a creator and with a potential user of copyrighted work, it is important to be careful about the scope of copyright. The "edges" of copyright protection can be unclear in many people's minds, so this can be an important area to pay attention to as a coach. Copyright protects original expression that is fixed in a tangible medium, which means, first, that unoriginal and unfixed expression is not protected. So a purely extemporaneous lecture is not protected, although, if there is an outline or notes, the lecture itself might be protected as a derivative work if it is recorded or written down. And work that is not original, such as a compilation of pure facts like a phone book, is not eligible for copyright.[11] It is sometimes important to help clients understand that just because they put effort into compiling a database of facts, they sometimes cannot claim copyright over that compilation. Facts are not subject to copyright protection, and there is no copyright granted for "sweat of the brow," although a compilation might be protectable in a rudimentary way if the selection and arrangement of the facts is sufficiently original. It is often the case, to take one example, that a researcher will want to use data from a previous publication in her own scholarship. Extracting factual data for reuse does not implicate any copyright protection, since facts are ineligible for protection, but reproducing an entire chart or graph might, because the selection and arrangement might qualify the work for protection. The issue of reusing such a chart as a whole will have to be resolved at a later point in the analysis, when coach and client discuss fair use.

Another way in which scope arises for copyright coaches is with the person who says they have thought of a great title for a book or a song, and wants to protect that title while the work is being written. This is simply not possible, since titles and short phrases are also outside of the scope of copyright. This situation also offers an opportunity to help clients distinguish between copyright and issues of plagiarism.

A final reminder about the scope of copyright is that works created by the U.S. government are not eligible for copyright protection. This is simply a policy decision made by the U.S. Congress,[12] and for copyright coaching, it usually comes up in situations where this principle, which many clients grasp in a basic way, has to be qualified; clients need to understand that copyright might still apply to government works from other countries and to works created by state and local governments. Helping to decide if a government employee was really acting within the scope of his or her employment when they created a work, or if it might be the work of a contractor who can receive a copyright and can even transfer that copyright to the federal government, can be a difficult task. An Environmental Protection Agency report about environmental hazards, for example, is very likely the production of a regular employee and therefore in the public domain, while the photographs in a national park brochure are much more likely to be the work of a contractor and potentially protected. This issue calls for coach and client to examine the specific circumstances as closely as possible.

Whether or not a work is in the public domain is the single issue that comes up most frequently when working with this first question, "Is there a copyright?" Often clients will confuse public availability with the public domain, thinking that because they can find something on the Internet, they must be entitled to use it without restriction. A copyright coach has to be able to help clients understand the more restricted nature of the public domain. This is where dates of publication become especially important, as does the situation regarding the copyright formalities in place at the time a work was published (if it was published). Since 1978 it has been true that books published before 1923 are without question in the public domain, and, beginning in 2019, that date has begun to advance, so that, each year, works that have been published for more than 95 years will enter the public domain. Unpublished works by authors dead more than 70 years also continue to become public domain. As for formalities, works published in the United States without any copyright notice before 1989 are public domain, as are works published in the United States between 1923 and 1963 for which the rights were not renewed, as was then required.[13] In short, the public domain is a technical aspect of copyright law, created by the various ways in which protection fails or lapses, even though it is not specifically defined or even mentioned within the statute.

Perhaps the most important principle to remember when working with clients on the issue of whether or not a copyright exists for a particular work is that ideas are never protected by copyright; they are in the public domain. When a second work borrows only ideas from a prior work, no infringement has occurred. This is important both for the creator, who should acknowledge borrowed ideas, especially in scholarly work, but does not need permission to use them; and for users, who are free to use ideas however they see fit. Several times, I have talked with clients who believed, as teachers or mentors, that because they had suggested an idea for research to a student or colleague, they were entitled to control the resulting work. This is not true, and it illustrates the point that ideas are "as free as air to common use."[14] Ideas of all sorts, no matter how they are expressed, are entirely available to be reused and re-expressed in new ways. It is the expression that is protected, not the ideas that underlie it.

When dealing with this general question of whether or not rights exist in a particular work, it is sometimes necessary to help the client get over some misunderstanding about the scope of copyright protection. One especially common error is the idea that there is some special category of "electronic rights" that are distinguishable from the rights that are specified for all copyright holders: to wit the exclusive right to control

1. Reproduction
2. Distribution
3. Public display
4. Public performance
5. Preparation of derivative works
6. Digital broadcast of a sound recording

Note that, with the exception of the final right, none of these exclusive rights are specific to particular formats or media. There is, in fact, no such thing as "electronic rights" apart from the application of these six exclusive rights to digital media. The origin of the misunderstanding, I believe, is the 2001 decision by the U.S. Supreme Court in the case of *New York Times v. Jonathan Tasini*.[15] So when a client raises this issue, often in the form of "we didn't get electronic rights as part of the donor agreement" for a specific collection, it is important to understand how to sort out the misunderstanding.

The *Tasini* case involved freelance authors whose works were published in the *New York Times* and then, at some later date, were republished in the

Lexis-Nexis database, as part of a digital collection of newspaper articles. The authors objected to the uncompensated republication of their works, and the *Times* defended itself by asserting that section 201(c) of the copyright law, which governs the copyright that a compiler/editor has in the collective work, gave them the right to "reprint" the works "as part of a revision of the collective work." To oversimplify a bit, the Supreme Court held that the republication in the Lexis-Nexis database, where the articles could be accessed individually and without the same context in which they appeared in the newspaper, did not qualify as a revision of the original collection. Such republication was also not mentioned in the contracts that the *Times* had with many of these freelance authors. Thus the Court found that the authors' copyrights had been infringed; not because they had some kind of special rights over electronic reproductions, but simply because a reproduction (which happened to be electronic) had been made outside of the rights granted to the *New York Times* either by contract or by section 201(c). *Tasini* can certainly stand for the proposition that contracts should be negotiated carefully and with as much foresight as possible, but it does not expand the scope of the exclusive rights in copyright or require that agreements make specific mention of "electronic rights."

This frequent confusion about electronic rights illustrates the ways in which our clients can misunderstand their own situations vis-à-vis copyright, often because of what they have read or heard about in media reports when important cases are decided. One of the most common tasks of the copyright coach is to help clients understand the true boundaries of the bundle of exclusive rights that the law grants as part of copyright. This issue of the scope of the rights can get pretty complex, and before we leave this first of our five questions, I want to consider a special area in which the scope of the exclusive rights has some unusual features.

OUR FIRST MUSICAL INTERLUDE

The application of the copyright law to music is a particularly fraught and difficult area, and we will have several occasions to address its special quirks. At this point, I want to make note of three aspects of music copyright that are particularly relevant when working with a client to consider the issue of whether a copyright applies to a particular musical work.

Musical works nearly always represent multiple copyright interests; at the very least, most musical compositions include rights held by the composer and the lyricist. These two individual bundles of rights, however, are often held together by a music publisher, either because the composition is treated as a work made for hire or by assignment. These rights, in the basic musical composition, are frequently licensed by a collective rights organization (CRO) like ASCAP, whose name—American Society of Composers and Publishers—accurately describes the rights holders it represents. Then, of course, when a musical work is recorded in some way, the performer will also hold rights in her performance. So when coaching a client about using a recorded song, it is necessary to account for these multiple rights—the rights in the underlying composition, which may be held by one entity, usually a music publisher, but which can themselves, in theory, be held by multiple rights holders—*and* the rights held by the performer.

The rights held by a performer also have a unique feature that can impact coaching; there is no broad public performance right in a sound recording. The law simply excludes sound recordings from the kinds of copyrighted materials that receive an exclusive right over public performance.[16] This results in the odd situation that musical performers simply do not get control over most of their public performances. So, when a radio station, for example, wants to play a CD over the air, they must clear the rights in the composition, through a CRO like ASCAP, but they don't have to pay any royalties to the performer or the record company. This is also the provision that allows covers of popular songs; the cover artist must, like the radio station, clear the rights for the composition but, again, does not need to compensate the original performer.

A further complication to this situation was added in 1995, when Congress amended section 106 of the Copyright Act to include a sixth exclusive right, which covers one specific kind of public performance for sound recordings, namely when the performance is transmitted digitally. Since that time, performers and record companies can enforce a right over digital performances, so various types of Internet radio do have to clear the rights for sound recordings (as well as for the compositions). This would also be true for the client who wants to use a popular song as background on a video that they will distribute on the Internet; they will have to consider the rights held in both the composition and the performance.

The final quirk about music copyright that belongs in our discussion about issues of scope has changed recently. For many years, sound recordings made before February 15, 1972, were simply not protected by federal copyright. In all other instances, federal copyright law preempted state protections, whatever they may be. But when sound recordings were brought into the scope of federal protection in 1972, that protection was not extended backward, and the exclusion of pre-1972 recordings from federal protection was continued by the 1976 revision of the copyright law.[17] In 2018, however, this part of the law was changed by the Music Modernization Act (MMA). Sound recordings that were made before February 15, 1972, are now protected by the same right over digital performances that is described above.

When working with a client who is interested in using older recorded music, there are now two consequences of this new law that may come into play. First, the situation for digital radio services has changed. Before the

MMA was passed, the pop band The Turtles, who had recorded some hit songs in the late 1960s including "Happy Together" (1967), which were regularly played on Internet radio services, had been suing Sirius XM radio in state after state in an effort to determine if state common law protection includes a public performance right that would force Sirius to pay Flo & Eddie a fee to broadcast their performance. These lawsuits have now been mooted by the MMA and a royalty would now be required.

The other change regarding pre-1972 sound recordings that the MMA has brought about is the fact that these recordings will now begin entering the public domain according to a revised schedule. Whereas the former situation was that none of this material would become public domain until 2067, there is now a graduated schedule for these materials. Sound recordings fixed before 1923 will now enter the public domain on January 1, 2021. For recordings fixed between 1923 and 1946, the term of protection is now ninety-five years plus an additional five, for one hundred years. If fixed between 1947 and 1956, sound recordings will get 110 years of protection (95 plus 15 years). Finally, the remaining sound recording that had not previously been subject to federal copyright law—those fixed between 1957 and February 15, 1972—will enter the public domain as originally planned, in 2067.

A FEW WORDS ABOUT INFRINGEMENT

Before we turn from our first question, about whether or not a copyright protects a particular work, to our second, which deals with licenses, it seems appropriate to discuss copyright infringement. Most clients, after all, consult librarians and other experts about copyright because they are afraid that they will commit copyright infringement and face legal consequences. So a coach must be prepared to discuss how courts will assess an allegation of infringement, although the coach's first job, of course, is to ensure that no such allegation is ever made in the first place.

Clients often begin with a very literal view of infringement, in which only literal copying is seen as potential infringement. For these clients, it is important for the copyright coach to explain that "substantial similarity" is the standard that courts use, a standard that is more inclusive than many clients expect, but also less inclusive than some fear. Courts are looking to see whether a reasonable person would find that the work accused of infringement was copied from some protected original. Is the accused work enough like the original that copying is a reasonable conclusion? It is very important to communicate this to those clients who believe they can use some original by redrawing it themselves, or by making minor alterations so as to "make it their own." These efforts—and many people believe in their efficacy—must be evaluated under the substantial similarity standard, which tells us pretty clearly that the result of these efforts, which is to create something as much like the original as possible, is unlikely to survive the real test that a court would use. We need to work to educate such clients that copyright protects content, not specific versions of that content, if they are substantially similar. For many of these clients, coaches need to move them through our five questions to number four, fair use, since that is where they will most likely find support for their efforts.

Another point about infringement that needs clarification is the idea of "de minimis" use. De minimis refers to a use that is so small or trivial that the law will not take notice of it.[18] Sometimes clients will try to convince the coach, and themselves, that the use they want to make of an original work is de minimis, but care must be exercised with this concept. If we look at cases where de minimis has proved a successful defense, they are usually situations where the alleged infringement is not central to the new work and is something most people would fail to notice. In *Gottlieb Development, Ltd. v. Paramount Pictures,* for example, a court found that a pinball machine that appeared in the somewhat blurry background of a three-minute scene in the movie *What Women Want* was too obscure and trivial to be actionable.[19] But this defense will not apply to many more straightforward uses, where fair use will be a better argument if the amount used is small and the use is educational. Also, de minimis can be unreliable. In music cases, for example, at least one court has held that de minimis simply does not apply to music sampling, while another jurisdiction has recognized the defense for the same situation.[20]

OUR SECOND QUESTION
"Is There an Applicable License?"

Turning to the issue of licenses is the second question to consider in our ordered list: "Is there an applicable license for the copyrighted work?" In this regard, it will be helpful to begin our reflections by focusing on the needs of a client who has created a work and is anxious to understand how copyright might help or hinder her planning. For the creator, the licensing question asks her to consider how she would like others to be able to use her work, and what uses she does not want to encourage. This is an excellent opportunity to discuss what "All Rights Reserved" means in the context of a specific work. It is fine to explain that a copyright holder is vested with six exclusive rights: reproduction, distribution, public display, public performance, the preparation of derivative works, and digital transmission of a sound recording, but the meat of the discussion should be about how those rights can help or hinder the client to meet her specific goals for her work. If she has composed a new song that she hopes to commercialize, these rights are important support for that goal. If, on the other hand, she has developed educational videos that she would like teachers to incorporate into a variety of different lesson plans, she will need to consider very carefully how she wants to convey the permissions she intends to grant to the audience for her work. This is where licensing comes in.

A license is simply a grant of permission to exercise a right that the licensor holds, and that the licensee could not otherwise take advantage of. When I tell my neighbor that he can walk across my property to get to the bus stop, I have granted a license, which can also be thought of as a promise not to sue for trespass. When a client decides not to license her work, the coach should explain that she will be solely responsible for all of the rights the law grants copyright holders, and that anyone seeking to exercise those rights will have to seek individual permissions from her or risk legal action. If she decides to sell those rights, permissions and litigation decisions will be in the hands of the new rights holder. She should also understand that uses that are outside the scope of the exclusive rights, such as private performance or display, uses authorized by specific exceptions, and fair uses, will still be available to the public. For a client who wants users to be able to do specific things with her work, or who does not want to be bothered by permission requests, a license is probably in order.

In many situations, the Creative Commons (CC) licenses will very effectively serve the needs of a client who is seeking to allow certain uses and not others. Most CC licenses include a requirement that the user attribute the original work properly, which is particularly important for many people in the United States, where the copyright law does not mandate attribution for most rights holders. Only the CC0 and Public Domain dedication licenses which are not really licenses, but more like waivers or mere statements about copyright status—do not include this "BY" element, which is the attribution requirement in all four types of CC BY licenses. A rights holder using a CC license also has two other decisions to make, or loci of control. She can decide whether to allow only noncommercial uses of her work (the NC term in the CC BY-NC license) or to permit commercial uses as well. This is often a good time to remind the client that non-licensed uses are not impossible; they simply require specific permission requests for each potential use. The rights holder can also decide to forbid derivative works entirely (the ND term in the CC BY-ND license), or to require that any derivatives be distributed with the same license as the original (SA, for Share Alike, in the CC BY-SA license). When a CC license does not include either an ND or SA term, all forms of derivative works are permitted.

Obviously, a discussion about using a CC license is a great opportunity for coaching, since a client must consider in detail what uses are important for her work and where maintaining control will best advance her goals. It is also important for the coach to convey that licensing, including the ability to use a CC license, depends on holding rights to the work in the first place. Sometimes our clients believe that, since CC licenses convey a public benefit, using them is an act of philanthropy to which no one could object. But it is potentially infringement to apply a license to a work that one does not hold rights to either as the creator, assignee, or subsequent licensee. CC licenses are a wonderful, powerful tool for rights holders to use to mitigate much of the fear that copyright generates for potential users, but they are not appropriate in all situations, and they don't relieve us of the need to do a careful and complete analysis of the rights situation when using the work of another.

Because licenses are a choice available to rights holders, users will often encounter licenses that affect how they can use specific materials. Consider the professor or graduate student who wants to share course materials with her class. Some of the works she wants to share may be licensed with a CC license; in that case, she just needs to verify that her use will comply with the specific terms of the license in order to proceed. Other materials she wants to use may be available on the Internet without a clear license. In those cases, she must assume that all rights are reserved until she has contacted the rights holder and been given permission. These are precisely the situations where it would be desirable for the rights holder to have considered users in advance and provided some kind of licensing statement on the website. The professor may also want to use some of her own publications, or materials found in library databases. For her own work, the professor will need to know, or find out, whether she transferred rights to a publisher and, if she did, what rights were licensed back to her. In other words, can she use her own work based on licensing language contained in her publication agreement, or must she seek permission from the publisher to use that work?

For materials found in library journal packages or databases, a license from a commercial provider will very often dictate permissible "downstream" uses. Faculty, students, staff, and, often, "walk in" members of the public are usually allowed to read articles and to download or print them under these licenses, as long as these activities are not done systematically or in bulk. Whether or not the license allows distribution to a class or to other members of a research group will vary a good deal and depends on the negotiations that took place between the library and the vendor when the resource was obtained. Of course, fair use will still apply (unless the license explicitly excludes fair use, which is a contract term no library should accept), so while addressing this question with a client, the coach may discover that she needs to move the discussion to fair use in order to fully examine the situation. If a license does not appear to permit the desired use, but does not specifically forbid it, fair use will be an option based on an analysis of the circumstances of the particular use in light of the fair use factors.

When working with a teacher who wants to use materials in a class, licenses can be part of a more comprehensive strategy for evaluating use. When there is uncertainty, several options are available—the teacher can use licensed works, consider fair use, substitute CC-licensed materials when possible, or ask for permission. Obviously, this is exactly the kind of situation where using our five questions, in their proper order, will be very helpful. To give a concrete example, I worked with a number of professors who were trying to move a course they had taught in a face-to-face classroom to an online environment, where it was intended for an audience of the general public. In the classroom course there were lots of illustrations in the lecture slides, which were authorized by a specific exception in the copyright law (17 U.S.C. §110(1)). But when the situation changed, and the class was no longer face-to-face, we had to look at the relationship between licenses, fair use, and permission. It was often difficult to find a rights holder for the images, so permission could only be sought sporadically. Fair use was certainly an option, but it depended on the specific use of the particular image. In many cases, licenses were the best option; we would seek to replace the image with an illustration either from a commercial image database where the license allowed, or we would seek a comparable picture that was licensed under a CC license. By seeking CC-licensed works, or other openly licensed materials, we were able to resolve quite a few problems.

As this discussion has indicated, it is often the case that a license is created by a contract that is primarily directed to a different purpose. Libraries license databases, for example, in order to offer a wide variety of resources to their patrons. But those licenses may also contain licensing language that seeks to control the uses that library patrons, such as faculty planning a course, can make of materials found in the specific resource. These contracts can be problematic, since the library often has no way to exercise control over, or even communicate the terms of the license effectively to, library patrons. From the perspective of the copyright coach, however, this is a reminder to look deeply into the source of the material that a client hopes to use in order to see where there might be a license that would clarify the situation. Another such situation arises when the client has created something using a software tool, and wants to exercise her copyright in some way. Occasionally, the license by which she obtained the software tool could dictate some terms of use that relate to the product created with it. This is becoming less common, but it is one more place where attention to licenses is important for the copyright coach.

The "publication agreement" is a special instance of this situation, in which a contract that intends to accomplish one thing—authorization to publish a journal article, for example—also creates a license that dictates the terms of use for other situations. In the digital environment, the licensing terms in a publication agreement have become vitally important as reproduction and distribution have become easier, and authors continue to feel ownership over their own works even after they have transferred copyright. Once it is signed, the publication agreement serves as an attempt to control this sense of ownership and to limit the ways an author can exploit the affordances of digital technology; that is, to compromise with the Internet and retain some level of the control that publishers exercised in the print era. Thus, many authors who wish to use their own work in new ways, such as in a learning management system like Blackboard, Moodle, or Desire2Learn, or by depositing it into an institutional or disciplinary repository, are confronted with some complex and problematic terms. Generally, these licenses depend on distinctions between versions of the article, distinctions about types of distribution, and embargos. Embargos, of course, are simply periods of time that must elapse after commercial publication before the author is permitted by the license to make specified uses of her work. The distinctions between forms of distribution can be harder to comprehend. They often allow distribution through a personal or individually maintained website, but not, for at least some versions, in a repository. Unfortunately, the technological infrastructure at many universities renders this distinction hard to apply, if not meaningless. So this is another point where the copyright coach may be called upon to help clients understand and apply licensing terms that impact potential uses, in this case of the client's own work.

From a copyright perspective, the distinctions between different versions of an article can be the most misleading ones. Publishers frequently divide the uses they are licensing back to authors based on whether the version used is the "preprint," which usually means the initial version before peer review, the "post-print" or final submitted manuscript, which is the version as revised after peer review, and the final published manuscript. The distinction between pre- and post-peer review generally makes sense to scholarly authors, but the difference between the final manuscript and the published version is often slight, and difficult for authors to understand. Publishers wish to maintain exclusivity over the "version of record," which has page numbers and is the version others will most often cite, but the difference between this version and the manuscript that the author sent in are quite often superficial. Thus, the coach will have to work to help authors understand this license term within their publication contracts. Also, it is important to understand that this distinction between versions does not indicate separate copyright in the different versions. Copyright protects content, and unless the different versions are substantially dissimilar, which is unlikely, one copyright protects all of them. Copyright is very flexible, and can be transferred or licensed in a wide variety of ways. With these publication contracts, the usual situation is that copyright is transferred in its entirety, but selected rights, often defined in terms of these different versions, are licensed back to author. Thus, the versions do not reflect different "bundles" of rights, but only the terms of particular licenses related to the overall copyright bundle at issue with a particular article.

Before we turn from licensing in general to special issues related to musical performances, we should acknowledge one other type of license that all of us encounter frequently: the terms of service (TOS) associated with many websites, especially various types of social media platforms. Most of us recognize that these TOS licenses are extremely complex and tend to limit our rights, as well as compromise our privacy and restrict our remedies against the platform proprietor. Such terms of service arise occasionally for the copyright coach, especially when a client wants to use some service that is intended for personal use in a classroom or other educational setting. As with all licenses, these situations require close attention to the terms presented and a careful examination of how the circumstances of the use mesh with those terms.

A SECOND MUSICAL INTERLUDE

Licensing is another area, like the kind and scope of rights that exist, in which music offers some unique situations, and requires the careful attention of a copyright coach. More than any other kind of copyright subject matter, music has developed a complex licensing culture, which is enshrined both in the law and in practice. An effective coach should be able to discuss compulsory licenses, blanket performance licenses, and the distinctive licensing practices related to so-called "grand" and "sync" rights.

The copyright law creates a number of compulsory licenses, which are licenses that are mandated by the statutory law. A rights holder cannot refuse these licenses, but usually is compensated for them according to a statutory scheme. Musical performance is perhaps the area most impacted by these compulsory licenses, which we already discussed when talking about the scope of the public performance right for music. Readers will recall that there is no general right over public performances for performers, so that musical covers can be made without authorization from those performers. But composers, lyricists, and publishers do have rights that are implicated by covers and all other public performances of their compositions. So, in order to foster experimentation and innovation in musical performance, a compulsory license for these rights in compositions was created in the law. This license created by law originated at a time when performances on player pianos and jukeboxes were becoming common, and it supported those businesses, which is why it is sometimes referred to as a "mechanical license." It also supported the radio industry, which used the mechanical license to gain authorization to broadcast compositions, and was not, and still is not as of this writing, obligated to compensate those who hold rights in the sound recording.

The compulsory performance license for sound recordings is created by section 115 of the copyright law and, for copyright coaches, it means that clients who want to use a musical recording for purposes other than digital broadcast, can pay a set fee to one of the performing rights organizations (PRO), such as ASCAP or BMI (Broadcast Music International). There is no need to seek permission from the music publisher as long as the fee is paid to the correct PRO; that is, the PRO that licenses that publisher's or composer's catalog. And, as has already been explained, there is also no need to seek permission from, or pay a fee to, the performer of the musical recording. For these transactions, the combination of a mechanical license for the composition, and the absence of a public performance right for the performance, simplifies matters considerably, as it was intended to do for various performance-based industries. The situation is complicated, however, by some of the quirks about music copyright discussed previously, including the digital broadcast right that performers now hold.

Performance rights organizations like ASCAP and BMI also offer blanket licenses for public performance of the music in their catalogs. With such a license, a music venue or a college campus can permit a wide variety of musical performances. By purchasing annual licenses from all the major PROs, a campus will gain the needed authorization, especially when considered in conjunction with the performance exceptions that we will discuss later, for its orchestras and bands, as well as for faculty recitals, student performances, and even visiting musical acts. Many questions that come to a copyright coach about musical performances can be answered by examining these licenses; they will eliminate problems in many situations, but their exact terms need close attention. For instance, the recording of musical performances is often permitted under these blanket performance licenses, but the specific parameters of that authorization may vary. Likewise, the licenses usually allow the broadcast of those recorded performances, but are quite restrictive about the venue for those performances. A campus-owned radio or cable TV station is probably permitted, but interpretations vary significantly on whether broadcasting a recorded performance on the college's YouTube station is permissible or not. This is an area for careful attention to details, and the coach may find it necessary to consult with the campus's general counsel or some other campus official who handles licensing.

Licenses in general are only effective for the specific rights to which they refer, such as public performance, and the specific terms and conditions they impose. In the case of public performance licenses, there are two significant gaps in the standard blanket license terms, which the copyright coach needs to be aware of. These performance licenses *do not* license the right to use sound recordings or other musical recordings in conjunction with a stage production or as part of a video. These two potential uses are licensed separately, and are referred to as "grand" rights and "sync" rights, respectively. So if a client wants to make a video using the song "It's Time" by Imagine Dragons as the soundtrack, the coach will need to direct her to the publisher or composer, since these entries usually continue to handle sync rights. The same is true for grand rights, if the client wants to use the music for a stage production.

To summarize and complete this picture of music licensing on a university campus, it might be helpful to look at multiple use situations for a specific song, and "It's Time" will work as well as any other. If the client wants to sing that song as part of a vocal recital, or wants to have the campus jazz ensemble perform it, only the blanket performance license is needed for authorization. The same is true if the CD is played at a party or dance. If the song is being used in a video or in a stage production, separate licensing of those sync or grand rights is required. Furthermore, if the performance of the song by Imagine Dragons is being broadcast on the Internet, a separate license covering the performer's right over digital transmission may be needed, and can be obtained from an organization called SoundExchange.

Music licensing is very complicated, as I am sure this quick attempt to summarize the issues has shown. It is an area in which the copyright coach must be sure to make careful distinctions for the client, and be realistic about his or her own capacity in the area. For projects that are highly visible, especially if they are not clearly related to the core teaching mission of the institution, referring the client to the campus counsel or to an outside counsel may well be the smartest strategy a copyright coach can adopt.

THE THIRD QUESTION
Do Any of the Specific Exceptions in Copyright Help?

In the text of the U.S. copyright law, the enumeration of the exclusive rights in section 106 is immediately followed by a brief section that codifies fair use. The remainder of chapter one, and the largest part of the law, are the specific exceptions, which usually constrain the scope of one or more of the exclusive rights, or explicitly permit some activity, often on the part of a specified group of users. These exceptions are a vital part of copyright's balance of private rights and the public good. Without them, copyright would fail in its constitutionally required purpose to "promote the progress of science and the useful arts."

These specific exceptions—all of the exceptions to copyright except for fair use—are very important in coaching situations, although they are sometimes overlooked. If a client's desired use of copyrighted material falls within the scope of a specific exception, they gain a degree of confidence that is seldom available when one relies on fair use. The exceptions tend to work like checklists where, if each condition is met, reliance on the exception can be very reassuring. Fair use, of course, is not a checklist but a balancing of factors used to analyze particular circumstances, so a decision about fair use is much easier to disagree on and to challenge. This may be why there is so much less litigation related to specific exceptions than there is over fair use. Fair use is immensely useful, but also subjective. So if—and it can be a big if—a client's desired use can be encompassed by the scope of one of these exceptions, that is an excellent direction for the coach to suggest.

There are fifteen sections detailing the specific exceptions in the copyright law (17 U.S.C. §§108–122), and those exceptions range from the quite simple to the extremely complex. Some, like the rules for rebroadcasting television programming on cable, seldom arise in copyright coaching situations. In the remainder of this section, I want to look at several of the specific exceptions that are most often useful to clients who are seeking to resolve a copyright question. But fair warning is due; these exceptions are very technical, and contain fine distinctions and complicated explications of the circumstances in which they apply. In what follows, I will examine section 108, the exception that allows libraries and archives to make copies for preservation and for lending to others, in considerable detail. I hope this will be a useful illustration of how the exceptions work, but readers who are not librarians, or who don't coach regarding library or archival uses, may wish to skim over the rest of this section.

There are usually three elements that make these particular exceptions specific. They always refer to some particular right or rights within the bundle of exclusive rights; they authorize defined activities, that is, the permitted uses of the specific right; and they authorize an identified group as the only users who are allowed to take advantage of the exception. So a copyright coach who has reached this question with a client needs to determine if the client is part of the authorized group, if the right they want to exercise is the one identified in the exception, and whether the activity falls within the scope defined by that exception.

Section 108 is the first of the specific exceptions, and it is a good place to start, since these three elements of an exception are clearly visible in it. Section 108 is often called the "library exception," and this title helps identify who the users are for whom the exception has been created. Those allowed to exercise the exception must be employees of a nonprofit library or archive, and the exception is only to the rights over reproduction and distribution. Thus, no one can rely on this exception for a public performance or to create a derivative work, for example. Within these fairly strict limits about who is authorized, and which rights are being excepted, the subsections go on to detail specific activities that are "not infringement" even though the enumerated rights in section 106 might suggest otherwise.[21]

There are two kinds of activity that fall within the scope of the section 108 exception: the preservation of materials held in a library or archive, and making copies one at a time to give to users. The provisions about preservation allow the library or archive to make three copies and distinguishes between how to do so for published and unpublished works. In both cases, the library or archive must have owned the original from which copies are being made and, if the material has been published, the library must also determine by "reasonable effort" that "an unused replacement cannot be obtained at a fair price." There is no definition of a "fair price," so this will be a judgment call on the part of the client. Note that, for the purpose of making and distributing preservation copies under this subsection, one must only look for an "unused" replacement; in other places within this exception the required search may have different parameters.

The two preservation-oriented subsections in section 108 also include a rather ambiguous provision that restricts the distribution of preservation copies that are in digital format, which cannot "be made available to the public in that format outside the premises of the library or archive." Many library and archive employees seem to focus on how the "premises of the library" are defined, so this may be an issue that a coach will need to discuss. But it is also worth considering who exactly constitutes "the public." Based on language used to define who is eligible to use the section 108 exception in the first place, it seems likely that according to the current language, the faculty and staff of an institution are not considered "the public" for the purpose of these rules.[22]

When a coach is helping someone navigate these two provisions, which allow making and distributing copies of materials, another issue is the "trigger conditions" that define the *published* material that may be copied. These conditions, which restrict the copying to materials that are damaged, deteriorating, lost, stolen, or obsolete, often raise the issue of what formats, exactly, are obsolete. Currently, people want to know if VHS tape is obsolete. The section itself tells us that a format is obsolete when the equipment needed to render it perceptible is no longer manufactured or reasonably available. This is an evaluation that institutions or communities of practice must make for themselves, since no central authority will declare a work obsolete. In the case of VHS tape, the issue seems to be very much undecided, but it is useful to observe that most VHS tapes, especially those that get heavy use, are certainly deteriorating.

As we progress further into section 108, the emphasis moves to making copies for users. This is the provision that underlies interlibrary loan practices, and all applications of it require that single copies which are made become the property of the user who requested them. In other words, libraries cannot use this provision to increase their collections or to build a library of copied materials "just in case" someone asks for them.[23] Copyright coaches should be aware of a couple of observations about these copies that are made and distributed to users who request them. First, library clients are often surprised to learn that, under subsection (e), they can make complete copies of works in their collections for a user. They must determine first, however, that a copy is not available at a fair price. Notice that here the law does not say "unused," so the user must presumably settle for any fairly priced copy before the library or archive can copy an entire work for them. Also, the provisions that authorize copies for users all require that a warning notice be displayed "at the place where requests are made," which today likely means on the library or archive's website. The text for this warning notice is specified in the Code of Federal Regulations, at 37 C.F.R. 201.14.

Finally, a coach helping a client understand these "copying for users" provisions of section 108 needs to address the role of the CONTU Guidelines. Virtually all librarians will know that there is a "rule" that says that a library or archive may not copy more than five articles from the same journal in a single calendar year. Like many things we all think we know, this is not strictly correct. First, the CONTU Guidelines were negotiated over forty years ago and do not reflect our current information environment. Also, the so-called "rule of five" is not really a rule; it is part of a set of guidelines which do not have the force of law, but which were an effort to define a provision in the law that says that interlibrary loan copying should not be systematic or a substitute for library subscriptions (see subsection 108(g)). It is at most a strong suggestion, not a rule. Finally, an accurate version of this suggestion is that a library should not request more than five articles from the most current five years of a particular journal title. That is, it is not any five articles from a journal title, but only articles from the most recent five years; older articles do not need to be counted. This guidance applies to the borrowing library, which makes sense since that is the institution that is able to decide when the number of interlibrary loan requests indicates that a local subscription is needed. So for libraries that choose to follow CONTU, it is the borrowing libraries that need to keep track of requests for the purpose of this rule, while the lending libraries that are actually making the copies need only have reason to believe that the borrowers are following this guidance.

One final aspect of section 108 that a coach should keep in mind when discussing the exception with a client is the remission of liability contained in subsection 108(f)1. That provision simply states that neither libraries nor archives, nor their employees, are liable for potential infringement committed by users who use unsupervised copying equipment provided by the institution, as long as that equipment has a copyright warning displayed on it. Unlike the warning required earlier in section 108, the text of this warning is not specified, so it can be pretty general, perhaps simply that the use of the machine—photocopier, scanner, and so on—is subject to the provisions of the U.S. copyright law and users are responsible to act accordingly. Copyright coaches should be sure that librarian or archivist clients understand the need for this warning, and should have it placed on all unsupervised equipment that can be used by patrons to make copies. It is also important not to police such equipment. The well-intentioned tap on the shoulder of a patron who seems to be copying too much can be problematic, since the librarian cannot know at a glance if the material is in the public domain, or is even being copied by permission, and trying to advise patrons in this way might actually create liability because it undermines the unsupervised nature of the machine.

FIRST SALE AND THE PERFORMANCE EXCEPTIONS

After this rather lengthy exposition of section 108, I hope the reader is more familiar with the structure of the specific exceptions and their application, so we can now treat several other exceptions more briefly.

The doctrine of first sale, found in section 109 of Title 17, acts like a boundary on a couple of the exclusive rights. That is, one way to understand first sale is as a limitation of the reach of the rights holder's control over distribution and public display. In fact, in other countries, what we call first sale is often called the doctrine of exhaustion because a simple exposition of the limitation is to say that the right over distribution is "exhausted" after the first lawful sale of a copy. For this reason, the new owner is free to redistribute that particular copy in any way. A lawfully obtained copy can be resold, lent, rented, or given away, but it may not, under the doctrine of first sale, be used to make additional copies, offered as a public performance of the work, or prepared as derivative works. First sale only applies to specific copies that have been lawfully obtained, and it only limits distribution and public display rights. After a first sale, the distribution right is exhausted and public display (of that copy) is permitted in defined circumstances. This doctrine thus authorizes a limited scope of otherwise infringing activities, and only for individual copies of a work. But its authorization is general—anyone can take advantage of it and, after the U.S. Supreme Court decision in *Kirtsaeng v. John Wiley*, all lawfully obtained copies are subject to first sale, regardless of where the copies were manufactured or originally obtained.[24]

An example of a situation where first sale is important to a copyright coach might arise when an individual or library is concerned about whether or not a personally owned copy of a book or video may be put on reserve or otherwise loaned out by a library. The answer, of course, is that it can be, since under first sale the owner may distribute the work in whatever way he or she wishes. First sale underlies all library lending activities, at least of print and analog materials. This is also the exception that permits used textbook sales for students, as well as the entire industry that sells secondhand books, videos, and records. Perhaps because it is so pervasive, first sale does not often arise in coaching situations, although it can be important to reassure clients about distributions that might seem outside normal practices, or in regard to materials that were obtained in unusual ways. Donated materials, for example, are certainly subject to first sale and are available for loan as long as there is no contractual provision to the contrary in any donor agreements.

First sale also allows the public display of copyrighted materials as long as the display is made only to people who are at the same place as the copy that is being displayed. So displays of books and paintings in libraries and museums are allowed because of this provision of the copyright law, but a digital display is not; doing that kind of display must rely on some other exception if it is permissible.

This restriction reflects a more general limitation on first sale; it clearly applies to print and analog copies of copyrighted materials, but its application to digital works is very much in doubt. In *Capital Records LLC v. ReDigi, Inc.*, a recent lawsuit challenging a service that was intended to facilitate the resale of digital music files, a judge in the Southern District of New York issued an order that held the doctrine of first sale could not apply to digital works, because all transfers in the digital environment involved copying.[25] Noting that whenever a digital file is transferred from one device to another, a new copy is made, Judge Richard Sullivan concluded that first sale, which has always been applied to transfers of the same copy, simply has no role in the digital realm. The Second Circuit Court of Appeals upheld this decision, and the logic that the court uses, while extremely literalistic, seems compelling. So copyright coaches need to be careful to warn a client who wants to transfer her thinking that relies on first sale into the area of digital works. For e-books, to take one example, any ability to lend digital files will depend on the terms of a contract between the vendor and the institution, not on the doctrine of first sale.

A very common issue that arises in copyright coaching is that of public performances of various types. Of course, when the performance involves musical works, and the institution has a blanket license from ASCAP and/or other performance rights organizations as described previously, some of these questions will be answered at an earlier stage in our framework for analyzing a copyright problem. But often the performance is outside the scope of such a license, or the institution has no license, so the coach must look next at the performance exceptions in section 110 of the copyright law.

When the question involves a performance in a face-to-face classroom, which is covered by subsection 1 of section 110, the coach's primary job is usually to convince the client to relax and accept that the law means what it says. Essentially, no permission for public performance is required if the performance (such as a film showing, recital, or reading) is part of a teaching activity that occurs within some form of instructional space. The language here is very broad—"teaching activity"—and clients often want to hedge this with rules of their own, such as the assumption that the law must only mean classes that are part of regular instruction, for example. But that is not the language in subsection 110(1). Since such requirements are imposed on online performances in subsection 2, it is clear that Congress was making a distinction, so it seems pretty certain that any form of teaching activity, not just formal parts of a curriculum, fall within this exception. Thus, no permission is needed for a very wide range of performances in such in-person teaching. Campus club activities, for example, probably can show films without permission, while a film screening that is purely for entertainment should be licensed. The coach will need to help clients recognize the wide scope of this exception, evaluate the particular activity in question, and then decide if the place where the performance is to take place qualifies as a "classroom or similar place devoted to instruction."

The parallel exception, in subsection 110(2), which is intended to authorize some performances that are transmitted to students over digital networks, is much more restrictive and quite difficult to apply.[26] As if to remind us that the specific exceptions work like checklists, where each element of the exception must be met in order to take advantage of the authorization it provides, subsection 110(2) imposes approximately a dozen different requirements for someone wishing to transmit a performance to online students. Some are either policy or technical requirements that the institution must meet, while others must be attended to by the individual instructors. For example, an institution must have copyright policies in place, as well as a secure network that is capable of authenticating users. The transmission must be part of the regular, mediated instruction of an accredited nonprofit educational institution or a government agency. The transmission must be restricted to enrolled students, and "reasonable technological measures" must be taken to prevent even authorized recipients from retaining or retransmitting the digital files. And instructors must pay careful attention to what they wish to transmit, since the exception normally does not allow entire works to be performed, only "reasonable and limited portions" of them.

The complexity of this performance exception has led to a couple of different reactions. Some institutions simply despair of being able to take advantage of the permission that Congress was trying to offer. Others have created some helpful guidance for instructors and schools to follow in order to ensure compliance with all of the requirements. The checklists offered by Louisiana State University (https://www.lib.lsu.edu/services/copyright/teach/index) and by the University of Texas at Austin (https://guides.lib.utexas.edu/copyright/teachactchecklist) are fine examples of these latter strategies, and may help some coaches realize that, in the right situation, subsection 110(2) can assist clients to achieve their goals for the use of copyrighted content.

The four specific exceptions discussed so far—the library exception, the doctrine of first sale, and the performance exceptions for face-to-face and online teaching—are the ones that a copyright coach in educational settings will need to discuss most often with clients. But there are others, so coaches should be prepared to look to other exceptions when the client's needs dictate. Among these remaining exceptions that deserve quick mention is subsection 110(4), which is another performance exception that covers a general range of nonprofit performances that are not being transmitted. When a client is looking to offer a performance outside of traditional educational contexts,

110(4) might be useful depending, of course, on the circumstances. Section 112 authorizes copying when necessary for other exceptions, including 110(2), so that a client will have some parameters within which to work when she needs to make ephemeral copies in order to teach online with a performance. Another rarely needed but potentially useful exception is found in section 120, which governs the use of photographs taken of architectural works. Buildings are subject to copyright, so photographs of a protected building are potentially derivative works that are within the ambit of control of the rights holder. But section 120 dramatically limits that control, in order to allow the photographer to make many traditional uses of the photograph. Finally, section 121 authorizes the copying and distribution of copyrighted works for use by people with visual disabilities. This can be exercised only by authorized entities, but the district court in the HathiTrust litigation held that libraries are such entities for the purposes of section 121, so this is something that a coach working with library clients needs to be aware of.[27] Indeed, all of these exceptions may come in handy in a copyright coaching session, and deserve more or less detailed attention from the would-be copyright coach.

FAIR USE

There is a real sense in which the five-question framework acts as a kind of funnel, guiding many of the issues that a coach is presented with toward fair use. Copyright coaches will find themselves at this point fairly often, after determining that there is a copyright to be considered, that no license determines the issue, and that the desired use does not fit within the scope of any specific exception. Fair use, which is listed first among the exceptions in the copyright law (section 107), is often the catch-all for questions that cannot be resolved by the first three steps, and it seems that this is intentional. Lawmakers in the United States have repeatedly chosen to leave most educational uses to the fair use analysis, rather than to create additional specific exceptions. Because there are relatively few court decisions regarding fair use in educational settings, we are forced to work by analogy when we look at cases. Mastering the fair use analysis remains vital for anyone hoping to coach copyright in educational settings.

The actual statutory instructions for a fair use analysis are surprisingly brief; section 107 is only a half-page long in the Copyright Office's publication of the law, and thus is one of the two shortest of the exceptions to the exclusive rights.[28] Depending on how one looks at it, this brevity may belie the importance of fair use, or it may actually explain why it is so important, and so frequently litigated. Fair use was originally judge-made law, and it is still intended to grow and adapt itself to changing conditions. It is short because the four fair use factors are intended to guide users and courts through a fact-driven analysis that depends on the specific circumstances of the use in question. The provision is short because almost everything about the analysis depends on those circumstances.

For almost anyone setting out to be a copyright coach, the four fair use factors should be very familiar: (1) the purpose and character of the use, (2) the nature of the original work, (3) the amount and substantiality of the portion used, and (4) the effect of the use on the market for or value of the original work. Although there are certain routinized ways of pursuing the analysis of these factors that courts have developed, they really just identify the specific kinds of information that should go into a determination about whether or not a use is fair.

But before we look at how these factors work, we should pause and consider the examples that the statute provides for the sorts of uses that might be fair use. Specifically, section 107 says that *"fair use of a copyrighted work . . . for purposes such as criticism, comment, news reporting, teaching (including multiple copies for classroom use), scholarship, or research, is not an infringement of copyright."* So the first thing a copyright coach should do when talking with a client who is asking about fair use is find out what, precisely, they want to do with the material they would be borrowing. Our courts have been very clear that these examples are not automatically fair use; a full analysis of the four factors is still necessary. Looking at how courts view them, one might say that these typical uses create a rebuttable presumption of fair use; if a use fits into one of those categories, there is a thumb on the scale in favor of fair use, but a full analysis of the factors can overbalance that thumb. In any case, knowing the intention of the user is vitally important, both for assessing the role of these examples and for thinking through the first factor in the full analysis.

The basic application of the four fair use factors by our courts has become rather mechanical over the years, and there are a few basic questions that courts tend to ask regarding the factors. For the first factor—the nature and purpose of the use—the normal starting place is whether or not the use is commercial. Courts have sometimes said, and occasionally still say, that a commercial use is presumptively not fair use, although the Supreme Court has rejected this presumption.[29] The other traditional consideration here is to look at those examples quoted above. If a court can squeeze the use into one of the exemplar purposes, the chances are good that the first factor will favor the user (normally the defendant) in the fair use argument, although, as I have indicated, this weight given to the examples from section 107 can be counterbalanced.

Most important to the analysis of the first factor, at least since the 1994 Supreme Court ruling in *Campbell v. Acuff Rose Music,* is a court's perception that the use is, or is not, transformative. We will discuss the notion of transformation in more detail shortly, but here we should note that when a use is found to be transformative, the odds that it will be held to be fair use increase dramatically. Nevertheless, courts continue to acknowledge, often citing a footnote from *Campbell,* that non-transformative uses may still be fair use.

If we put the issue of transformativeness to the side for a moment, the remaining fair use factors are also often subject to a rather mechanical analysis. The second factor, which is about "the nature of the original work," usually asks whether or not the original has been published, and where it is located on the continuum from factual to highly creative works. An earlier Supreme Court case, *Harper and Row v. Nation Magazine* 471 U.S. 539 (1985), indicated that the unpublished nature of the original work weighed strongly against the possibility of fair use, but that conclusion was explicitly reversed by Congress in 1992 when a line was added to section 107 stating that no such presumption should be applied. And the issue of fact versus creative seems to generate more heat than light, since it is possible to argue from both directions about many works. Is a work of history creative or merely factual? Which words best describe educational materials? Unfortunately, debates like this dominate discussions of the second factor, which has the potential to be very important for fair use, but in practice usually carries little weight.[30]

The third factor, regarding the amount or substantiality of the portion used in relation to the original, is also treated in summary fashion by many courts. Often the third factor is tied to the first, when courts pose the question of whether the amount of a work used is appropriate to the purpose. As we will see, this relationship takes on even greater import when we consider transformative uses. For now, we should note that there really is no bright line percentage, number of words, or length of a segment that one can rely on and be "within" fair use. Clients often come to a coach with a strong notion that only 30 seconds of music or only 500 words of text can be fair use, but the coach must firmly disabuse clients of this idea. The amount that will be acceptable as fair use will always vary based on the overall circumstances of the use. It should be clear that borrowing even 30 seconds of a song would be treated with great suspicion if it were used without permission in a TV commercial, while the use of much more than that in a parody or other attempt to comment on the song will receive a more favorable hearing. The ongoing case over electronic reserves, brought by publishers against Georgia State University and defended by that school as fair use, is a good example. The judge in the case found that the use was not transformative, and held that a maximum of 10 percent or one chapter was allowable. The Eleventh Circuit Court of Appeals rejected this bright line rule, while agreeing that the use was not transformative. Nevertheless, in a subsequent decision, the district court judge did not venture too far from her original percentages, although she was a bit more flexible, because the nature of the use is such that a larger amount would surely impact the issue of market harm.[31] Thus, it is important that the third factor always be kept in context, and evaluated in light of the other factors.

The fourth factor, which looks at the potential market harm or loss of value for the original work if the use is permitted, is probably the most difficult and contested factor. At one time this was certainly considered the most important factor, but that has changed some since the ruling in *Campbell*, when the Supreme Court held that all of the factors should be evaluated and weighed in light of the purpose of copyright law.[32] Approaches to this part of the fair use analysis still diverge widely, however. Some courts will look at all potential markets, and hold that there is harm whenever a rights holder might have realized licensing revenue. Other courts look only at actual sales of the original, or only at markets that are traditionally exploited by the particular type of rights holder. Courts not only disagree about which markets are relevant to the assessment of market harm, but they are also split over how deeply they will consider potential harm versus a real, documented loss of revenue. Sometimes a court will ask what would happen if the use in question were to become general; a question that usually tilts the fourth factor away from fair use and is really quite unrealistic in many instances. With this amount of volatility in the fourth factor analysis, the coach really must discuss the amount of risk carefully with the client and try to evaluate the client's tolerance for such risk.

These traditional questions in the fair use analysis take on a different character when the court examines the issue of transformation, as most have done since the *Campbell* decision. That analysis, as has already been suggested, begins with the first factor, since it is fundamentally about the nature of the use and the new work that has been created, but it has a significant impact on a court's consideration of all of the fair use factors. The basic question that courts ask is whether or not something new has been created through the challenged use, with a different purpose, meaning, or message. Sometimes the new thing is a changed work, such as the parody song that was at issue in *Campbell*, or the collage artworks being evaluated in *Cariou v. Prince*.[33] In other instances, what is new is the purpose to which the original has been turned. For example, in *A. V. v. iParadigms*, the Fourth Circuit held that student essays being submitted to the TurnItIn anti-plagiarism service were repurposed to such a degree that there was transformative fair use even though no changes were made to the original texts themselves.[34] Finally, courts have found that creating new meaning can also be a transformative fair use, as in the case of images from Grateful Dead concert posters that were used, without license, in a published book recounting the history of the band. In finding that the use was fair, the Second Circuit held that new meaning was created when the posters ceased to be concert advertising and became, instead, "historical markers."[35]

In all of these cases, once the courts held that the use was transformative, the other factors were analyzed in light of the transformative purpose. The creative nature of the original became less important, arguably because the use itself was so creative or transforming. The amount of the work used was evaluated in light of the purpose, so that the question was not, objectively, "was a little or a lot used?" but rather, "was the amount used appropriate to the purpose, and was neither too much nor too little to have the transformative effect?" Finally, the discussion of market harm becomes much less important, since courts generally do not find that the rights holder is entitled to control any market for transformative works.

The fair use analysis in general is very friendly to educational use, and nonprofit educational use will almost always at least sway the first factor in favor of the user. The preference for transformative uses is particularly beneficial for scholars and teachers. When parts or excerpts from protected works are incorporated into teaching materials or new scholarship or teaching, they are very often transformed by being subjected to criticism and comment. When assessing a potential transformative fair use, the coach and client should work through three questions: Does the incorporated material help me, the user, make *my* new point? Will it help my readers or viewers to understand *my* new point? Is the amount used appropriate, and is neither too much or too little, to make *my* point? It should be clear that these questions, which are fundamental to analyzing transformativeness, are also essentially questions about good pedagogy. In short, the more the incorporated material serves the purposes of good teaching or good scholarly analysis, the more likely it seems that it is also transformative fair use.

Coaches and clients should embrace this advantage for nonprofit educational and scholarly uses, but they should not abuse it. Not all uses at a school or university are automatically transformative; the questions should be asked and answered in good faith.[36] And it is important to remember that a use might be fair use even if it is not transformative. In that case, the other fair use factors become more important, and the coach should guide the client through the issues of the nature of the original, the amount used, and the possible market harm very carefully. To repeat, what is essential here is a responsible and documented analysis of the particular facts and circumstances surrounding the specific use. There are no shortcuts in fair use, but when it is used responsibly, it is an immensely beneficial provision that was specifically designed to help teachers, researchers, and scholars.

Fair use is vitally important for good copyright coaching; it is the go-to play that helps our clients navigate the "game" they are involved in. It is very complex, but it is also the point where most of the situations we encounter will be resolved. To become comfortable coaching about fair use, there is no substitute for reading cases, learning all the different situations where fair use has been evaluated, and seeing how courts apply the parts of the analysis to the particular facts before them. In this section, I have added more citations to my discussion of fair use than in other parts of this chapter; this is so coaches can easily find and read the cases. Another valuable resource is the catalog of fair use cases provided by the Stanford University Copyright and Fair Use Center.[37] A similar catalog has recently been created at the U.S. Copyright Office, called the Fair Use Index.[38] These will help coaches see the overall shape of the field before them and point them to cases that they should read in detail as they encounter particular circumstances. Also, there are multiple resources that can help the coach become more familiar with how to think about fair use and which can also serve as places to refer clients, so that the latter can develop the facility to make those good faith, fair use judgments that are the key to navigating so many copyright situations. I particularly like the materials at the Columbia University Copyright Center, including the Fair Use checklist.[39] I must note, however, that this checklist is not an infallible determination about fair use; it is merely a guide to thinking about fair use and a way to document that thought process. The checklist, and all of the other resources now available to copyright coaches in the academic world, are useful ways to improve one's thinking about fair use, but they can only act as guides; they do not replace thoughtful assessment of the facts and situations that confront the specific client.

YOUR LAST RESORT
Asking for Permission

Asking permission is a last resort only because it comes at the end of the framework for thinking through a copyright issue. After the coach and client have determined that there is a copyright protecting the work in question, that no license supports the planned use, that no exception does either, and that relying on fair use is outside of the client's comfort level, the question that remains is "who can we ask for permission to use this work?" Permission has a significant advantage in this schema, since it can cover any planned use and it provides a degree of certainty that can be lacking at other stages. In fact, sometimes a client will seek assistance specifically for finding a rights holder to ask for permission, and it may be determined to proceed in this way even if there might be other options. I once worked with a student who wanted to write a play based on several of the short stories of Ernest Hemingway. As I listened to him describe his project, I began to talk with him about transformative fair use. But the young man was adamant that he wanted permission from the Hemingway estate, because of his respect for Hemingway. While I do not agree that relying on fair use is disrespectful, my client was very determined, so we set about seeking permission for his creative endeavor. I will return to this story as we continue to unpack the process of permission.

Before we turn to issues involved in finding the correct rights holder, we should briefly consider how to ask for permission. Clients often worry about the format of the request and the response. Do they have to send a formal letter to the copyright owner, or can an e-mail request suffice? Must the reply be a signed letter? How should it be recorded, if at all? Since in most cases the client will be seeking a nonexclusive license, which means a license that allows her to do what she asks for but does not preclude others from being given the same permission, the license does not actually have to be in writing. Chapter 2 of Title 17, which governs the ownership and transfers of copyright (and so bears study by any copyright coach), tells us that a transfer or exclusive license must be done via a signed document. By implication, a nonexclusive license does not have to be a signed piece of writing at all. Nonexclusive licenses can be verbal, or even implied by law or by the actions of the licensor. While this gives our clients some room for informality, however, I always advise that clients obtain some form of written confirmation of the permission they are seeking. An e-mail, properly stored and retrievable when evidence of the license is needed, is fine for most purposes. Although it is possible to record a license with the Copyright Office, to do so requires either a signed document or a sworn affidavit and, again, in most cases is not necessary.[40]

The most important part of any request for permission to use a copyrighted work is the scope of the license that is sought. Care should be taken that the proposed use is described as fully as possible. Permission is only helpful, after all, if the use the client wants to make of the work is fully covered by what the rights holder has granted. Often the rights holder will depend on the request to define the scope of permission, so coaches should work with clients to provide a full description of the use. It is important to include who the audience for the use will be and whether there will be commercial gain, simple cost-recovery, or no charge at all associated with the use.

In my opinion, it is also important to be persistent when asking for permission. Sometimes a first message to the rights holder may go unanswered, or may be answered with a knee-jerk "no." This happened with my young man seeking to use some Hemingway short stories; our first request was summarily refused, and my client was devastated. We tried again, however, putting strong emphasis on the academic and noncommercial purpose of the use. To our relief, this second request was granted; apparently we had simply needed to be very clear about what was intended, and a little bit stubborn.

In some cases, persistence means asking the same rights holder repeatedly until one gets a reply, or even considering an alternative pathway to make the request. When there are several potential rights holders due to inheritance or joint authorship, for example (more about these possibilities shortly), it might be wise to try a different person or entity. Sometimes, of course, there will simply be no reply from the rights holder. I always recommend trying to contact the rights holder at least three times, but at that point the potential returns are definitely diminishing. Eventually it can become clear that permission will not be forthcoming, so it is necessary to reenvision the project, possibly using different materials that are in the public domain or openly licensed, or to revisit fair use. The knowledge gained about the unwillingness of a rights holder to reply to a request for permission may, after all, strengthen the reliance on fair use somewhat because it indicates the absence, or failure, of any licensing market. And courts have been consistent in holding that a request for permission in the first place does not undermine future reliance on fair use.[41] In all cases, of course, requests for permission should be polite and respectful; they should also be directed to the right person, insofar as due diligence in searching has yielded results. We now turn to this issue of finding the correct rights holder.

Copyright is owned immediately by the creator of the work, except for works that are made for hire; in those cases, the employer of the creator, which is often a corporation or other institutional body, owns the rights in the work from the moment of creation. If the rights holder is an individual, her rights will pass by inheritance when she dies. Recall that copyright always outlives the creator, since the term of protection is the life of the creator plus seventy years. Rights do not dissolve away early, even when there are no obvious heirs. The law defines heirs in nearly every situation, even if a will left by the rights holder does not. So, a client seeking permission must assume that rights persist until the end of the copyright term, and should search for rights holders accordingly. In the case of my student client and Ernest Hemingway, we knew we needed to locate a literary executor, and that is who ultimately gave us the permission my client needed. In other cases, permission might be sought from a surviving spouse, children, siblings, or even the parents of a creator. Each situation will be different, and it is sometimes necessary to start with what you believe is the most likely rights holder, and politely ask in the request to be referred if the person addressed does not, in fact, hold the necessary rights. Book or journal publishers, of course, are often the rights holders because the rights have been transferred to them, and these organisations usually have identifiable contacts for permission, although sometimes it can be hard to get an answer from a publisher, especially when no licensing fee is contemplated.

Work that is made for hire is the big exception to the rule that copyright vests immediately with the creator. When a work falls within the definition of work made for hire (defined in 17 U.S.C. §101), the law recognizes the employer, not the creator/employee, as the rights holder from the moment of creation. Subsection 201(b) of the copyright law simply creates the legal fiction that the employer, in work made for hire situations, is the "author" of the work. So as a client prepares to seek permission, he may need to know the circumstances under which a work was created. Was the creator acting within the scope of her employment when she authored the work? Or perhaps she was as an independent contractor, in which case some very specific information—or a direct query to the creator—may be needed to determine who the rights holder is. In some of these cases, it will be pretty clear that something is a work made for hire, while in others it may be necessary to ask and hope for referrals when needed.

A very common situation, of course, arises when the creator is an academic and the coach and client must decide whether the work they are interested in is owned by the scholarly author or by her institution. In this case, I believe that it always makes sense to start by asking the academic author. In a great many cases, universities have specific policies that disclaim work made for hire; that is, the policies say that, at least for traditional scholarly works like monographs and journal articles, the authors hold the rights (which, of course, they often assign to publishers) despite the work made for hire rules in the copyright law. For this reason, coaches will do best to recommend starting with the author, since that is the person who is most likely to know the policies of her own institution and to also know, of course, if she has assigned the rights to anyone.

There are exceptions to this general advice to start with the creator of a work when the work is a form of scholarship and the author is employed by a college or university. Many institutions claim ownership over data, for example, since the institution is often responsible to a grantee or government agency for the integrity of the data and the conclusions drawn from it. Likewise, institutions may claim rights in measurement scales, psychological assessments, standards, and similar materials created by their faculty. But while these exceptions to any broad assumptions about academic policies regarding work made for hire add some complexity, they do not change the basic advice to start with the creators and let them guide your inquiry, since they are best placed to understand the situation.

Of course, if the creator is an employee of the U.S. federal government, the inquiry should not have gotten to this point, since any work created within the scope of that employment will be in the public domain. If a refresher on this point is needed, please review the discussion under the first question in our framework.

One of the most common authorship situations that must be understood when considering who to ask for permission is that of joint authorship. The principle here is simple and very important; when a work is created by two or more people, each of the creators holds an equal share of the rights, and each one can exercise those rights without consulting the others (although they must account to the other creators for any profits). It doesn't matter if one author did 90 percent of the work and the other did only 10 percent; each of them will hold a 50 percent share in the rights. Practically, the important point for dealing with a jointly created work is that each author is entitled to grant permission for a use. This is part of what it means to say that each author can exercise his or her rights independently of the others. Permission from one author is sufficient, even if the work in question was written by five people working together. It is sometimes sensible, in cases where it is practical, to get permission from all or from as many creators as possible. Doing so reduces the potential for difficulties later on, since everyone who could raise an objection has already agreed to the proposed use. But as a matter of law, it is not necessary; permission from one rights holder in a jointly authored work is legally sufficient.

The most common situation for joint authorship, of course, is the scholarly article written by several people, who can sometimes form quite a crowd. A reminder about this situation may be in order here. In most cases, the rights in these articles have been assigned to a publisher, so it doesn't matter if there are seven authors or seventy; the publisher will be the entity with which to begin the process of obtaining permission.

Sometimes asking permission is a straightforward task, and sometimes it is simply impossible. But it can also be circuitous, leading client and coach through several discoveries and changes of direction. I was once working with a professor who wanted to use a short excerpt from a book written by a colleague in an online class he was teaching. On his behalf, I went to the author who was, as I say, another professor at the same institution, and asked his permission, since his name was listed as the copyright holder on the title page of the book. This author told me he was happy to let his colleague use the excerpt in the way I had outlined, but he asked me, as a courtesy, to inform his editor at the publishing house. When I spoke to that editor, she was surprised and unhappy since, according to her, the contract between the publisher and the author, while it did leave copyright in the author's hands, designated the publisher as the sole agent by whom permission could be granted. The author had either not understood this, or he had forgotten. In any case, the publisher's representative was less than pleased by the situation, although in the circumstances, where I had already spoken with the author/copyright holder, the publisher did not raise any objection to the use. I recount this story simply to illustrate that the search for permission sometimes depends on information that simply is not available, at least at the start, and thus it can take some unexpected turns.

RESOURCES

The tools that can help a copyright coach track down the person or entity from whom permission should be sought are, unfortunately, neither common nor comprehensive. The process of searching, which often fails and then has to move in a different direction, will actually be quite familiar to librarians who do reference work; it is necessarily iterative and can be quite frustrating. Usually the coach will start with whatever source the client used to locate the material she wants to use. Books and articles offer an easy place to start, since they normally supply both the author's name and the publishing house, although, as my previous story indicates, that may not be the end of the search. For online resources, various methods for finding metadata will be needed, depending on how the resource is structured and presented. Google searching, of course, can be quite fruitful. Our colleague librarians, of course, who are specialists in specific subjects at issue, can really help guide these searches. When looking for the rights holder of an image, reverse image searches using Google or an application like TinEye may help the coach find other instances of the same image and therefore offer more possibilities to locate metadata.[42]

Beyond these general resources, there are a few databases that can help with specific types of materials. The records of the U.S. Copyright Office, naturally, hold a lot of information. Unfortunately, they are complicated and difficult to search, and only a small percentage of the records are searchable online, though the office is working continuously to increase the number that are digitized and the quality of retrieval. So those records, at copyright.gov, are usually a good place to begin. The Stanford database of copyright renewal records, although limited to monographs, will also sometimes help a coach determine who the most recent rights holder was.[43]

More specifically, the Harry Ransom Center at the University of Texas, Austin, maintains two databases that can be quite helpful when seeking rights holders. The WATCH file (Writers, Authors and Their Copyright Holders) is a good first stop when looking for a literary estate or other rights holder for twentieth-century literary figures. It was the WATCH file that led my young dramatist client and me to the literary estate for Ernest Hemingway.[44] The Ransom Center also offers a database to help people who are looking for copyright holders and who discover that a company they were looking for is no longer in business. This database, called Firms Out of Business (FOB), lists known successors in interest for defunct companies that held copyrights. Since this can be a difficult problem when seeking a rights holder, FOB is a very useful resource.[45]

Sometimes all of these resources still don't yield the name or contact information of a rights holder, or else a putative rights holder who is contacted by the coach or client simply does not respond, even to multiple inquiries. These situations are the result of "orphan works," which are works still protected by copyright, but for which there is either no known rights holder or no practical source of permission. The situation around orphan works is very complicated and, like so much in copyright, depends heavily on the circumstances of individual works. Some resources that can help a copyright coach understand these situations are found on the Copyright Office website where there is a study of the problem, some proposed legislation that was introduced into Congress several years ago but not adopted, and a more recent (2015) report on "Orphan Works and Mass Digitization."[46] There is also an excellent article on "Solving the Orphan Works Problem for the United States" by David Hansen, Pamela Samuelson, and others that can help a coach contextualize the problem and understand the alternatives.[47]

The key point about orphan works has already been made in our discussion about an unresponsive rights holder; when faced with a true orphan work, where obtaining permission is simply impossible, that fact provides an additional data point for the fair use analysis. Thus, when the coach and client hit this apparent dead end, they should push their analysis back to fair use and reconsider its possible application. Now that they know that market harm is less likely, since there is no one to grant permission or collect a licensing fee, a borderline argument for fair use may swing in a more acceptable direction. This decision belongs to the client, of course, since he will be the party at risk, and his level of risk tolerance (or that of his institution) must be determinative. Unless and until Congress acts to resolve the problem, however, the client should at least be given the facts about the potential impact of orphan work status on the consideration of fair use.

A BRIEF NOTE ABOUT CIRCUMVENTION

In 1998, Congress adopted the Digital Millennium Copyright Act (DMCA) in an effort to update the copyright law for the digital age. While its relative success is a matter for debate, one aspect of the law has created an additional consideration for copyright coaches but does not fit neatly within our framework—the anti-circumvention rules now found in 17 U.S.C. section 1201.[48] This provision forbids "circumventing a technological measure that effectively controls access to a [copyright-protected] work." In other words, it makes it an act of infringement to copy or otherwise gain access to a work by breaking a digital lock, including various types of digital rights management. Copying a DVD that is protected by the Content Scramble System (CSS) is a common example of the kind of circumvention of technological protection measures that the DMCA is intended to prevent. There are numerous exceptions, however. For instance, the librarian of Congress is directed by the law to declare, every three years, certain "classes of works" for which circumvention will be permitted, in order to mitigate the potentially draconian impact of the law on socially beneficial uses of copyrighted materials. In fact, one of the exceptions that has persisted through several rounds of this triennial rulemaking permits exactly the kind of activity mentioned above—copying CSS-protected DVDs when the purpose of the copying is to use short segments of a film or video for certain types of educational activities.

The issue of circumvention cuts across all of the steps in our framework for considering a copyright issue, so wherever the analysis lands when working with a particular client, the coach will need to ask an additional question—does this use involve disabling or circumventing any technological protection measures? When it does, the coach can guide the consideration of several options. First, look at the exceptions to the DMCA that are currently in force—they are published in the Code of Federal Regulations—and consider whether any of them authorize the use. If the client will be depending on a specific exception in the copyright law, the coach should also look at 17 U.S.C. §112. This section provides authorization for certain types of ephemeral copies that are needed to take advantage of some of the specific exceptions, in spite of anti-circumvention rules. Of course, if the analysis has reached the point of asking for permission, a license or grant of permission will permit the necessary copying, so the anti-circumvention rules will not be a problem.

Finally, if the client is relying on fair use, it will be necessary to consider how that fair use interacts with the anti-circumvention rules. Unfortunately, there is no clear guidance for this consideration. By the express terms of section 1201, it seems that anti-circumvention rules do not apply if the use for which the circumvention is necessary is a fair use.[49] Some courts have taken this path, holding that for a circumvention of technological protection measures to be a violation of section 1201, the underlying use must also be infringement. Fair uses, of course, are not infringement. But other courts have applied the anti-circumvention provision without regard to any "nexus" with copyright infringement. As long as this split among U.S. courts persists, coaches will need to discuss the anti-circumvention issue carefully with clients. If the fair use case is very clear, and the use is localized and noncommercial, a client may feel safe relying on fair use to also permit circumvention. But uses that are likely to catch the attention of potentially litigious rights holders, such as those that involve widespread distribution, might require more caution. It is possible that a client would be well advised to consider seeking permission because of the risk of violating the prohibition on circumvention, and only return to fair use if the search for a rights holder is unsuccessful and indicates a lowered risk.

CONCLUSION

We have taken quite a long path through the framework of five questions for analyzing any copyright issue. As I said at the beginning, these questions each seem straightforward, but none of them is easy. At each stage, painstaking analysis is needed to help a client find the best option. The five-question framework provides the copyright coach with a game plan, but every game, of course, is different. The game plan still requires careful attention by the coach and client to specific circumstances, developing situations, and individual goals. And it requires practice. The would-be coach needs to practice with this game plan on several levels. Coaches should practice reading cases, especially about fair use, in order to understand the nuances of how courts think about copyright and then balance the different incentives for creation. Coaches need to practice discussing facts with potential clients in order to become adept at eliciting the right information from the client to address each question. Finally, and above all, the copyright coach must practice thinking in terms of the game plan we have built, since it provides a structured approach to copyright issues that can help the copyright coach achieve success in this work.

I want to close with a reminder. Clients often come to us quite stirred up about copyright issues. Usually they are deeply engaged in a project and have been brought up short by a sudden concern over some potential copyright violation. They may joke with us about going to jail, but it is clear that quite often they genuinely fear the potential consequences of getting things wrong. Yet at the same time that we work with these nervous clients, we are well aware that thousands of copyright-related activities are taking place in our libraries and on our campuses that never come to our attention, and never result in complaint, litigation, or liability. As we seek analogies from copyright case law, we cannot fail to notice that very little of it arises from an educational context. The entertainment and technology industries are where the money is, and thus where copyright conflict is generated. By and large the stakes, in the broadest view of things, are simply not that high, even though they may be very high indeed for the individual clients we work with. I believe that the five-question framework is an important and useful way for a copyright coach to assist those who come asking for help. But we need to recognize that, while we must work with our clients to resolve their specific issues, some perspective is required. Working in education, we are simply not in the vortex of copyright risk; indeed, we are often favored actors in the courts and in Congress. So we need to help our clients, and ourselves, to maintain a balanced perspective on risk and liability, while still striving to do what they believe is the right thing, ethically and legally.

NOTES

1. Roscoe Pound, *The Lawyer from Antiquity to Modern Times* 5 (West, 1953).
2. It is worth noting that, to the best of my knowledge, no action has ever been taken by courts or state bar associations to discipline librarians for the unauthorized practice of law. The need for care is borne not from fear of such liability, but out of our professional commitments as librarians.
3. The standard way to cite a legal provision is by the number of the title within the U.S. Code, followed by the section number. The copyright law is Title 17 of the code, and the definitions section of it, for example, is cited as 17 U.S.C. §101. All sections of the copyright law cited for the remainder of this chapter will be in this form, in the text.
4. See the interesting discussion from the Harvard Law School about the distinction between the case method and the case study method at https://casestudies.law.harvard.edu/the-case-study-teaching-method/.
5. Referring to *Kelly v. Arriba-Soft,* 336 F. 3d. 811 (9th Cir. 2003).

6. These five questions are fairly common among copyright specialists. I first learned to employ them from Peggy Hoon, who was, at that time, the scholarly communications librarian at North Carolina State University, and is now director of copyright policy and education at the Louisiana State University Libraries. Hoon offers a version of these questions at https://www .lib.lsu.edu/services/copyright/teaching/5steps. Another version, based on work I did with my colleague Lisa Macklin from Emory University, is found in several places, including this site from Kansas State University: https:// www.k-state.edu/copyright/docs/CopyrightFramework.pdf.

7. Notice ceased to be required for copyright protection as of March 1, 1989.

8. This is the language used in 17 U.S.C. §102(a).

9. At U.S. Copyright Office, "Registration Portal," https://www.copyright.gov/ registration/.

10. Registration of a published work is timely if it occurs within three months of publication, while a rights holder in an unpublished work can seek statutory damages if registration occurred prior to the act of infringement. See 17 U.S.C. §412.

11. The Supreme Court ruled on this specific matter in *Feist Publications, Inc. v. Rural Telephone Service Co.,* 499 U.S. 340 (1991).

12. The policy is enacted by 17 U.S.C. §105.

13. This brief discussion summarizes the major ways that works rise into the public domain, but it is an oversimplification. For a fuller treatment of these various rules, one of the best resources is Peter Hirtle's chart on "Copyright Term and the Public Domain," at https://copyright.cornell.edu/publicdomain.

14. The phrase comes from an 1918 Supreme Court case, *International News Service v. Associated Press,* 248 U.S. 215 at 250. The entire sentence is worth noting here: "The general rule of law is, that the noblest of human productions—knowledge, truths ascertained, conceptions, and ideas—become, after voluntary communication to others, free as the air to common use."

15. 533 U.S. 483 (201).

16. See the details of 17 U.S.C. §106(4), where sound recordings are not included in the subject matter to which the public performance right applies.

17. This situation is again the result of an exclusion from protection. Section 301 of the current copyright law preempts state common law protections, but there are some specific exceptions, which include pre-1972 recordings, as explained in subsection 301(c).

18. "De minimis" is derived from a longer Latin maxim, "De minimis non curat lex," which can be translated as "The law does not concern itself with trifles."

19. 590 F. Supp. 2d 625 (S.D.N.Y. 2008).

20. Compare *Bridgeport Music, Inc. v. Dimension Films,* 410 F. Supp. 2d 625 (6th Cir. 2005) with *VMG Salsoul v Ciconne,* 824 F. 3d 817 (9th Cir. 2016).

21. The language used in each of the specific exceptions is "notwithstanding the provisions of section 106."

22. Subsection 108(a) tells us that libraries and archives that wish to use the exception must be "open to the public," or at least allow outside research to have access to their collections. This use of the word "public" seems to clearly indicate that it does not refer to the regular users of the facility, including the faculty and students at the university served by the library or archive.

23. On the other hand, it should be noted that the two preservation portions of 108, subsections b and c, do permit copies to be made for the purpose of deposit into another library or archive. So one of the three permitted reproductions can be placed in the collection of a different institution, which naturally serves the interest in preserving especially rare or at-risk materials.

24. See 568 U.S. 519 (2013).

25. See the Memorandum and Order granting partial summary judgment by Judge Richard Sullivan, March 30, 2013, available at https://ia800604 .us.archive.org/12/items/gov.uscourts.nysd.390216/gov.uscourts.nysd .390216.109.0.pdf.

26. This subsection was amended in 2002 by the Technology, Education and Copyright Harmonization Act, also known as the TEACH Act. So reference is often made to the TEACH Act, as in the checklists mentioned below, but the legal requirements created by that act are found in subsection 110(2) of Title 17.

27. See the *Authors' Guild v. HathiTrust* case (755 F.3d 87 (2d Cir. 2014)) for language indicating that libraries are allowed by law, and are even encouraged, to make copies for the blind and visually disabled.

28. "Copyright Law of the United States," Circular 92, U.S. Government Printing Office, 2011, p. 19.

29. In *Campbell v. Acuff-Rose Music,* 510 U.S. 569 (1994), for example, the Supreme Court held that a commercial parody of a famous song was a fair use. In fact, most well-known fair use decisions do involve commercial uses, for the simple reason that those are the uses most likely to provoke a lawsuit. So the presumption that commercial uses cannot be fair use is clearly erroneous.

30. See the article by Robert Kasunic, "Is That All There Is? Reflections on the Nature of the Second Fair Use Factor," *Columbia Journal of Law & the Arts* 31, no. 4: 101–41. This article is also available at www.kasunic.com/Articles/ CJLA%20Kasunic%20Final%202008.pdf.

31. This case was originally *Cambridge University Press, et al. v. Patton, et al.* and is designated 1:2008cv01425 in the federal courts system. The name of the case has changed to *Cambridge University Press et al. v. Becker, et al.* because of a change in the leadership of the Georgia Regents. A second appeal in the case is pending before the Eleventh Circuit at this writing, after the district court judge ruled a second time when the case was remanded back to her by the appeals court.

32. See Neil Weinstock Netanel's article "Making Sense of Fair Use," at https:// law.lclark.edu/live/files/9132-lcb153netanelpdf.

33. 714 F.3d 694 (2d Cir. 2013).

34. 562 F.3d 630 (4th Cir. 2009).

35. *Bill Graham Archive v. Dorling Kindersley, Ltd.,* 448 F.3d 605 (2d Cir. 2006).

36. It is worth noting that the copyright law, in subsection 504(c)2, exempts employees of a nonprofit educational institution or library from the greatest part of the potential liability for copyright infringement—statutory damages—when they had a good faith belief that the use in question was fair use. Thus, an honest evaluation is important and serves the interests of the client even in a situation where a court ultimately decides that the decision about fair use was incorrect.

37. Stanford University, "Copyright and Fair Use Center," https://fairuse .stanford.edu/case/.

38. U.S. Copyright Office, "Fair Use Index," https://www.copyright.gov/fair-use/.

39. Columbia University, "Copyright Advisory Services," https://copyright .columbia.edu/.

40. The detailed requirements for recordation are found in 17 U.S.C. §205.

41. See, for example, *Campbell v. Acuff Rose Music,* discussed above, and *Bill Graham Archive v. Dorling Kindersley.*

42. TinEye can be found at https://www.tineye.com/.

43. Stanford Libraries, "Copyright Renewal Database," https://exhibits.stanford .edu/copyrightrenewals?forward=home.

44. The WATCH file is found at http://norman.hrc.utexas.edu/watch/. It is perhaps worth a word to finish the story of the student who wanted to write a play based on several Hemingway short stories. We did obtain permission, and the student wrote a powerful work as his senior honors project at Duke University. He kindly invited my wife and I to the opening night, and afterwards he asked me what he needed to do to move this work from a student project to a commercial enterprise, which serves as a reminder for coaches that clients sometimes change their vision for a proposed use partway through a project.

45. University of Texas at Austin, Harry Ransom Center, "Firms Out of Business," http://norman.hrc.utexas.edu/watch/fob.cfm.

46. See U.S. Copyright Office, "Orphan Works," https://www.copyright.gov/ orphan/.

47. David R. Hansen, Kathryn Hashimoto, Gwen Hinze, Pamela Samuelson, and Jennifer M. Urban, "Solving the Orphan Works Problem for the United States," *Columbia Journal of the Arts* 37 (2013), https://academiccommons .columbia.edu/catalog/ac:169934.

48. The DMCA, 12 Stat. 2860 (1998), amended half a dozen provisions of Title 17 and added several additional sections. For additional information, see https://www.copyright.gov/reports/studies/dmca/dmca_executive.html.

49. See 17 U.S.C. §1201(c).

JILL BECKER
and ERIN L. ELLIS

2

Integrating Copyright Coaching into Your Instruction Program

A S LIBRARIANS AND MEMBERS OF THE ACADEMY INCREAS-ingly encounter users who are creators, contributors, and consumers of information, we are often tasked with answering a broad range of questions related to copyright and fair use. Course assignments at both the undergraduate and graduate levels often involve the transformation or repurposing of content—from film and music projects to mixed media art collages, to the more traditional paper or presentation. Learners across our campuses—faculty, students, and staff—are working at the intersection of information literacy and emerging areas of scholarly communication. We have a significant role in helping these communities understand the value of information—their own information and that of others—as they pursue their scholarly and creative endeavors. The Association of College and Research Libraries' (ACRL's) "Framework for Information Literacy for Higher Education" clearly states that learners should develop their capacities in copyright and the ethical uses of information.[1] Librarians are uniquely positioned to guide learners through the practice and acquisition of this set of information literacy skills. Establishing the most effective way to provide this guidance—to a variety of groups and individuals with a variety of questions and needs—is the challenge.

First, let's consider how copyright education is currently provided at your institution. Is it provided as part of an instruction session? Through an online tutorial or video? Maybe you have opportunities to work with freshmen orientation classes, or perhaps you teach an in-person or online multi-week course. But whatever your opportunities are, would you say that they are opportunities to *coach* copyright? We discuss coaching as a pedagogical approach that is focused on addressing a particular problem or need, whether real or contrived, for the purposes of instruction. Coaching offers the opportunity to continually ask clarifying questions and to address the broad complexities of copyright and rights in a way that our usual teaching opportunities don't always provide. Coaching is thus an integral part of any copyright education program. But *coaching* copyright requires time—time to develop and account for a variety of contexts and scenarios, and time to understand some of the nuances of copyright law. Coaching also requires more time, since coaching usually takes the form of a one-on-one conversation with an individual who has a specific need. In this form, coaching echoes the characteristics of the consultation process. Librarians with instruction or reference desk experience know that sometimes our students and faculty don't know what they don't know and may not ask for what they really need when their inquiry begins. The same applies in copyright coaching. There are many complexities to the topic, so it is critical that consultation take place and that individual, unique details be considered when creating responses to these particular inquiries. Consultations require deep listening, developing rapport, reflection, and balancing the inquiries of the client with the expertise of the consultant.[2] In this chapter, the authors will look at copyright education in academic libraries and discuss its place within the ACRL "Framework for Information Literacy for Higher Education" (the Framework), and the opportunities to integrate its "Information Has Value" frame in particular. Additionally, the authors will discuss coaching's role in consultation and instruction, its overlap with high-impact educational practices, and examples of potential strategies and teaching scenarios for your copyright coaching program.

COPYRIGHT EDUCATION IN INSTRUCTION PROGRAMS

A look into the literature concerning copyright instruction reveals examples of familiar pedagogical approaches, but there are few that explicitly describe or include the concept of coaching. Most typically, copyright instruction is offered through an online tutorial or course module, as a one-shot introductory overview, as a workshop or workshop series, or as an online or in-person course. There are challenges to applying traditional approaches to copyright education, however, because there is often little or no opportunity for personalization or consultation. And the challenge with personalizing copyright education (and engaging in a more defined coaching model) is that it's difficult to scale. That's why so much copyright education comes in pedagogical packaging that is convenient: the online module or tutorial, for example, or an orientation-level introduction in a course. These are convenient and efficient ways to deliver content. These modes offer opportunities for awareness-raising and exposure to copyright concepts, but they have significant limitations if the content isn't developed as a *result* of coaching or isn't delivered *alongside* coaching. Also, importantly, these modes don't provide much opportunity for true coaching—to individualize content, to emulate real-life scenarios, to provide occasions for deep analyses, and to ask clarifying questions. So although they are convenient, these pedagogical approaches to topics of copyright and fair use may actually confuse learners or leave them feeling unsure. We must remember that copyright issues are complex, and most individuals are not actively engaging with copyright and fair use issues on a day-to-day basis. So without an opportunity for true coaching or consultation, individuals may be prone to apply their limited understanding inaccurately or inappropriately, or attempt to solve future problems with guidance they received on another issue entirely. Simple exposure to information literacy concepts is rarely sufficient, and instruction librarians will know this from their experiences with one-shot sessions intended to teach first-year students how to search databases. Without consultation and without defining a particular or individual need, the content is not readily retained and the learning outcome goes unmet. This is especially true for copyright and fair use education. There is a danger in implying that there are simple, generalizable answers to copyright questions Overview or one-shot sessions—regardless of the audience—often oversimplify complex issues and frequently imply that there are strict, inflexible rules that people must abide by, regardless of situation, and ignore the nuances of individual cases. Asynchronous, online instruction is particularly problematic in this regard because there are limited opportunities for personal, individualized engagement and conversation about these complexities. Pre- or post-instruction coaching is critical in order to provide this personalization and to address specific questions and needs.

Workshops get us a little further in terms of coaching possibilities. Workshops (stand-alone or as a series) provide more of the much-needed time to develop contexts and work through individual or real-life scenarios. There is usually a way to make use of workshop time to effectively provide copyright content while also providing personalized coaching. As with many instruction attempts, timing is everything. Though scaling workshops is often relatively manageable, determining when, where, and how often these workshops are offered is a critical decision since, ideally, these should be offered at a critical point of need for learners.

Multi-week or full courses offer the best opportunities to engage learners in tailored, coaching experiences; they are also, however, the most difficult to scale, if they are a realistic option at all. Nevertheless, multiple meetings throughout a course—however it's delivered—give ample opportunity to coach learners through the complexities of copyright and to employ engaging, active pedagogies that personalize the content and provide time to acknowledge the nuances of copyright and fair use considerations. There are lessons to be learned from those who have attempted copyright instruction in the full course format. For example, in her article "Copyright for Undergraduates: Lessons Learned while Teaching a Semester-Length Online Course," Tammy Ravas describes her approach to developing and delivering a semester-long copyright course and shares the course's week-by-week structure.[3] She utilizes case studies as the basis of the course—an active, high-impact learning approach—along with online discussions. But despite having the benefits of a full, sixteen-week course, Ravas still encountered challenges. Primarily, these emerged as a result of the course being fully online. The online environment is challenging when it comes to active learning, but particularly with copyright education there are significant limitations. The asynchronous nature of that environment just doesn't lend itself well to coaching, questioning, and consultation.

In their book chapter "Theft of the Mind: An Innovative Approach to Plagiarism and Copyright Education," Clement and Brenenson describe a curriculum and learning outcomes that they implemented as a first-year student seminar course.[4] Their curriculum approached copyright education as a series of experiences for the students and not in terms of compliance and consequences. This provided the opportunity to engage students in the many gray areas of copyright and fair use scenarios, placed students in their roles as consumers and authors alike through role-playing, and allowed opportunities to discuss the uncertainties around real-life, "stripped from the headlines" copyright situations. The benefits of a face-to-face, semester-length course are obvious in the authors' success with this course, which provides a model for copyright education programs that integrate active learning and coaching.

COACHING AS A HIGH-IMPACT PRACTICE

What distinguishes coaching from our usual instruction is the focus on and consideration of a particular, individualized need. Let's consider the differences between reading a book about pitching, hearing a lecture about pitching from a baseball player or coach, and practicing actual pitching techniques on the mound. Obviously, the actual pitching practice offers more opportunity for individualized, context-based coaching and qualifies as hands-on active learning. Advice and motivation are provided at the point of need. The combination of coaching and practice has immediate and real-life application, and is reliant on a relationship between the coach and the athlete. Pedagogical strategies that emphasize a coaching approach utilize role-playing activities, real-life scenarios, and mock debates. These strategies personalize the content and put students in a variety of positions—creators, contributors, distributors, and consumers. Approaching copyright education within a *coaching* framework provides significant opportunities to personalize issues and problems and allows for recalibration on both sides—those of both the coach and the learner—based on the details and ambiguities of a given situation. It has often been suggested that individuals learn best when learning is problem-based, hands-on, and active.[5] Using principles from constructivism, problem-based learning begins with an authentic problem or task and utilizes a scaffolded approach to build skills and knowledge that are built upon previous skills and knowledge. These approaches are particularly useful in copyright coaching and education opportunities. Utilizing complex, open-ended questions or scenarios that put students or faculty into role-playing or mock debate situations provides a real chance to coach within a context, address ambiguities firsthand, test assumptions from multiple perspectives, apply possible solutions, and practice higher-order thinking skills—which are critical elements of the Framework. This can be achieved in a variety of instruction venues, but coaching must be an integrated part—either in planning and preparing for instruction content, within the delivery of instruction (when time can be made available), or in a post-instruction opportunity.

By now, most academic librarians are familiar with high-impact educational practices because their institutions design curriculums and programming that support student persistence and retention. High-impact practices (HIPs) include first-year seminars and experiences, common intellectual experiences, learning communities, writing-intensive courses, collaborative assignments and projects, undergraduate research, diversity and global learning, service learning and community-based learning, internships, and capstone courses/projects.[6] Academic librarians play a role in these practices through both their physical spaces and their information literacy instruction programs.[7] For example, group study rooms and other library spaces allow for completion of collaborative assignments and projects and finding credible sources for a research paper occurs during a hands-on information literacy session. A review of selected literature on HIPs found that while information literacy competencies (as librarians understand them) are often included in high-impact practices, the literature does not refer to these skills and competencies as information literacy.[8] HIPs place an emphasis on collaborative problem-solving, transferrable skills, and the real-world application of learning. Copyright education is best provided in this way, too. Working through actual, real-life problems with learners is a tremendously effective way to relay the nuances of copyright while also answering real questions. While we know that one answer will not address all future situations, we know that working through known problems and discussing possible solutions that have appeared in case law will likely result in some transferability of copyright skill.

And we wouldn't be discussing copyright questions if we didn't know that there are real-world applications and needs for answers. Copyright is a real-world problem and one that many learners never consider without prompting. Regardless of need and regardless of how copyright instruction is delivered, learners must be given the opportunity to apply their knowledge in order for meaningful learning to occur. Copyright education lends itself perfectly to this kind of active, coaching approach.

COPYRIGHT COACHING OPPORTUNITIES IN THE FRAMEWORK

Copyright is clearly reflected in the ACRL "Framework for Information Literacy for Higher Education" through both its "Information Has Value" and "Scholarship as Conversation" frames. "Information Has Value" includes explicit language regarding both a legal and ethical understanding of intellectual property, and "Scholarship as Conversation" recognizes an ongoing scholarly conversation that builds upon the work of others in creating new knowledge. Additionally, the Framework shifts our thinking of students as merely consumers of information, to creators of information as well. Empowering students in their roles as creators of information is not something born out of information literacy; it is an undercurrent of high-impact practices as well. If one of the goals of HIPs is the application of learning to real-world situations, one method for achieving that goal is to create assignments for students that require the real-world application of learning. Often, this application of learning to a real-world problem results in the production of new knowledge. In these cases, knowledge production *is* the pedagogical approach. Furthermore, when students use the many online publishing tools that are available for both creative and collaborative endeavors, their class projects become publishing activities. Librarians encounter knowledge creation projects all the time. We see them when we consult with faculty on library instruction sessions, and we hear about them as "best practices" through the teaching centers on our campuses. These encounters are opportunities for coaching copyright.

One HIP that has a natural overlap with librarians' work is undergraduate research. Here is our best opportunity to work with students throughout each step of the research process. It is a natural fit with our tried-and-true "finding sources" instruction, but it also allows for more advanced learning as we help undergraduate researchers write literature reviews, collect and manage their data, and ultimately publish their own research. A recent study by Riehle and Hensley sought to understand undergraduate researchers' perceptions of scholarly communication and found that these students "could not accurately address copyright and author's rights as applied to their scholarship," that they "rarely receive specific guidance but instead follow leads of problematic data management practices," and that they struggle to determine the impact of the research.[9] All of our librarian readers are thinking, "We can help with this!" and yes, we can, but it can't be accomplished through a one-shot instruction session, and it can't be accomplished through an online tutorial. Riehle and Hensley suggest that their findings represent an opportunity to support student researchers, and this is true, and in many cases we already do. But a real opportunity to scale our coaching lies in the overlap with the HIPs occurring on our campuses. The authors ask, as more institutions increasingly integrate HIPs as part of the undergraduate experience, will those coordinating these programs "understand the importance of supporting students' information use and scholarly communication-related issues relevant to their roles as knowledge creators?" Anecdotally, and through our one-on-one consultations with faculty on their assignments, we know the answer is frequently no. The first step to overcome this is to develop partnerships. What happens next is coaching. This is true in all of our information literacy efforts, not just formal, undergraduate research experiences. We coach and consult with faculty and instructors all the time to develop relevant, point of need, outcome-based instruction. We coach and consult with them through assignment design, scaffolding, and setting students up for success. Working with faculty and instructors to develop problem- and scenario-based, real-life instruction opportunities in the realm of copyright serves two purposes: we design meaningful instruction and coaching opportunities for students, and we provide an opportunity to relay copyright content to faculty and instructors, too. When copyright coaching occurs during these types of instruction-related consultations, it is focused not only on the anticipated needs of the students, but also on the faculty/instructors' need (though they often don't know they have one).

STRATEGIES AND SCENARIOS

Since consultation is already part of many librarians' job responsibilities, it is within those conversations where we are most likely to find copyright coaching opportunities. Coaching needs to be focused on the unique needs and desired outcomes of the client/learner. This should feel similar to our approach to teaching and preparing for library instruction. When instruction librarians end up coaching copyright, it is not often because of a copyright-related question. Instead, it comes about because the librarian recognizes an eventual overlap with students' knowledge creation. When we consult with faculty in preparation for library instruction, some questions to ask them (or at least have in the back of our minds) might be: What do you want your students to produce? What can they learn about their own rights and responsibilities as part of the production process? While faculty may begin by relaying the information needs of their students (e.g., ten scholarly sources for their final project), the copyright coach's role is to listen for clues indicating knowledge production. While librarians may still provide assistance to students on where and how to find and evaluate information, they may also provide resources related to information ownership as it pertains to the students' writing and creative works that result from their completion of course assignments.

Let's consider how copyright education is a part of your instruction program. If it is not already there, you should include copyright education as part of your overall information literacy curriculum. This can and should take a variety of forms. The first form is through information literacy instruction. You can utilize the "Information Has Value" frame to develop learning outcomes for your instruction program that include copyright. The Framework provides language in its knowledge practices and dispositions that are easily translated into learning outcomes. You will see examples of this language in the scenarios below. These learning outcomes should be written at both the program level and the individual assignment or library instruction session level. To supplement face-to-face instruction, you can create topical resources on copyright such as LibGuides, handouts, videos, and interactive tutorials. These resources can be embedded throughout a course or assignment in order to scaffold copyright skills. The availability of these resources can help instruction librarians as they consult with faculty to negotiate the time spent on these topics in an already full course schedule. We, as librarians, also need to model good copyright and fair use practices in our own materials such as presentation slides, handouts, and other instructional materials. You can include appropriate Creative Commons licensing on all of your instruction materials. And finally, if your library offers for-credit classes, you should consider adding a course dedicated to information creation and copyright.

Your copyright coaching program should be a part of your instructional program, and will be more successful if you work and consult directly with faculty and other campus instructors. Copyright education should be in the minds of librarians as they work with faculty and campus partners to integrate information literacy skills. You should look for opportunities to discuss the "Information Has Value" frame as you negotiate assignment design and instruction sessions. As with instruction consultations, you should start by asking what exactly students are being asked to do. It is possible that the faculty member doesn't recognize the copyright issues at play when they design assignments. Positioning students as experts in role-playing or scenario-based assignments are immensely effective, encourages critical thinking, and is a valuable instructional opportunity when you work with faculty and their courses.[10] This practice often results in the outward-facing knowledge creation that lends itself to copyright questions. Unfortunately, the copyright implications inherent in these types of assignments seem to rarely be discussed (at least in our experience) in curriculum development opportunities that take place on our campuses. Librarians can take on the responsibility for "closing the loop" for students as creators of information by coaching them on their end product—and in this way, students begin to take a small part in scholarly conversations with an understanding of their rights and responsibilities as knowledge producers.

It is helpful to keep a "store of examples" consisting of scenarios for discussion with students and assignment examples to share with faculty and instructors. If your library has incentivized opportunities for information literacy integration, you should make one offering that is specific to copyright. For example, you can assist faculty in developing a copyright assignment that includes appropriate Creative Commons licensing so that it may be adopted for use by other instructors. Finally, identify opportunities to provide workshops that can help develop individual students' understanding of copyright concepts, and which can also assist faculty and instructors' efforts to help their students understand these concepts. Remember, coaching is a truly effective way to relay the nuances of copyright and fair use, but it must be purposefully integrated into your copyright education program and information literacy activities and outcomes.

In the spirit of real-world and scenario-based learning, let's walk through three coaching copyright scenarios that could be integrated into your instruction or could help you identify opportunities for copyright coaching on your campus and within your library. We offer these as possible teaching tools, but also as food for thought as you determine the activities and outcomes of your copyright education program.

SCENARIO 1

In my role as a librarian, I recently attended a training session for university staff and faculty who teach a first-year experience course. Part of the training was to introduce a new assignment (an annotated bibliography) that would be included in all sections of the course. The program coordinator had piloted the assignment in her own class, and she offered to provide examples of student papers to help instructors with grading their own assignments. At the suggestion of her supervisor (whom I had advised before on fair use and instructional materials), she contacted me for guidance on the legal and ethical considerations concerning sharing students' work with other instructors. She knew enough to understand that she needed to get permission from the students, and she had searched online for an example of a permission form. For the most part, the permission form she shared with me was good. It referenced U.S. copyright law and FERPA, it provided students with options as to where their work would be shared (e.g., Blackboard, course website, course reserves, etc.), and it gave students the option to include their name with their work or leave it anonymous. At the end of the form, before the signature, was the following statement, "I will identify any copyrighted content I did not create and which is not fair use so that my paper/project may be properly restricted to distribution only within the campus community." This final statement on the form gave me pause. The form was intended for first-year, first-time students enrolled in an orientation seminar. I myself had been involved with curriculum development for this course for six years, and I had taught this course as the instructor of record ten times. Because of this experience, I had two concerns with this statement: first, the curriculum for this course does not include instruction on the attribution of sources in general, let alone any discussion of copyrighted content; and second, the reality is that students, especially first-year students, will not understand the nuances of fair use. This means.that they are likely to sign the form without really understanding what it is that they are signing.

Since I had a hunch that the form needed revision, I brought it to one of my copyright colleagues for review. She agreed with my concern regarding the final statement and recommended that the wording be changed to read "I will identify any copyrighted content I did not create and include appropriate attribution." And to add a final statement stating "I represent that this submission is my own original work and that my project does not, to the best of my knowledge, infringe upon anyone's copyright. I also represent and warrant that this submission contains no libelous or other unlawful matter and makes no improper invasion of the privacy of any other person." In addition to discussing how to revise the wording on the form so it would be appropriate to the purpose, I brought up the point with my first-year experience colleague that it was likely that the instructors themselves did not understand the concept of fair use. The majority of individuals who teach these courses are student affairs staff who do not regularly have teaching responsibilities. They don't usually have a background in education or curriculum and likely have never considered fair use in this course or any other one.

In consulting with my first-year experience colleague, I raised these points and suggested that this might be a good instructor development workshop in the future. She agreed, and we are now in conversation about holding the workshop for instructors. In this scenario, I played the role of both client/learner and coach. I was coached by my copyright colleague on how to best respond to the first-year program coordinator, and I coached my first-year experience colleague. I now have the additional opportunity to become a coach to other instructors through a future workshop. This scenario reaches multiple audiences. The first audience is my first-year experience colleague, a campus partner responsible for implementing an HIP (first-year seminars and experiences). The second audience is the instructors who teach the first-year course, and the third audience is the students enrolled in the first-year course. In my role as coach, I need to consider all of these audiences, my learning outcomes for each, and how this fits into my copyright coaching program.

When my first-year experience colleague approached me with the permission form, it was my recognition of the overlap between program needs (sharing students' work to assist instructors with their own teaching and grading) and the eventual needs of the students that prompted my coaching. I wanted to ensure that students were provided with the information they needed to make an informed decision about how and where their copyrighted works were shared. When I workshop with the instructors who teach the first-year experience course, my end goal will be to equip them with enough information about copyright and fair use that (1) they will apply appropriate fair use considerations to any information they are sharing with students in their teaching capacity, and (2) they will know how to explain the permission form to their students in such a way that the students can make an informed decision.

SCENARIO 2

The second scenario begins with an e-mail from a librarian who was unknown to me, but who referenced an application for an award that I had submitted the previous year. In the message, the librarian asked me if I would be willing to write a brief summary of the work referenced in my application and, if so, allow it to be included in an open-access book. Thrilled at the prospect of being contacted to contribute to a book, I responded by asking about a deadline and how lengthy a summary was needed. In response, an individual in the book publisher's marketing department contacted me. Their response included a link to a "case study draft" that referenced my institution by name. This "draft" was, in fact, word-for-word plagiarism of my award application. I was shocked. Not only was their "draft" my original copyrighted material, but the "draft" was already being promoted and was available for downloading as part of the book without any attribution. At no point had I transferred copyright or given permission to use my work. This publication was using my original expression without my permission and this was copyright infringement, and besides, asking for permission after the fact is not good practice. It concerned me deeply to know that a publisher that trades in information literacy content—and was promoting an open-access publication—didn't seem to understand the ethical use of information, which is a basic tenet of information literacy.

To be sure that I had a full understanding of my own rights and that my response would be written as such, I sought counsel from the scholarly communications experts in my library, one of whom is a copyright lawyer. They confirmed that yes, copyright had been violated and yes, plagiarism had taken place. They advised me on the correct terminology to use in my response and reviewed multiple e-mail correspondence to ensure the language was appropriate. In this scenario, I was coached by my expert colleagues to make the decision that was best for me. They both asked me early on about my desired outcome (an excellent question and coaching strategy), and while the thought of my work being included in the publication was tempting (who doesn't enjoy an invitation to publish?), the practices of this particular publisher were dishonest to the point that I didn't want my name associated with what I knew were questionable publishing practices. Ultimately, I requested that my copyrighted content be removed entirely and not be included in the publication. This scenario highlights the importance of coaching within the librarian community and knowing when we have reached the limits of our own knowledge and require coaching to move forward in our professional decisions.

SCENARIO 3

We've all heard some variation of the saying, "If you give someone a hammer, everything is a nail." This phrase implies an overreliance on a familiar strategy and is often used to describe new learners as they develop their problem-solving skills, but it can also apply to understanding copyright and fair use. Years ago, I cautioned an instructor against scanning chapters from books and posting them to his Blackboard course for students to use. At the time, I did not know this individual well and I myself was not very well-versed in fair use considerations. I cautioned him that his practice might not be fair use and that he could only share a certain percentage of the work for his posts to be considered fair use. He asked me what that percentage was and I said, "I think it is 30 percent." Admittedly, I didn't know as much about fair use at that time, and I now know that "black letter" rules like this aren't the best approach or are accurate in all situations. But the point in this scenario is that this individual continues to use the 30 percent suggestion as a hard-and-fast rule applied to all things he wants to consider fair use, and he often quotes this percentage to other instructors. Examples such as this are useful as we consider the idea of "coaching copyright." In many cases, an individual will identify a solution to one copyright problem and then continue to apply that same solution to all copyright issues, when in fact he may need coaching in many different areas. Earlier in this chapter, we discussed that working through problems and discussing possible solutions should result in some transferability of skills. In this scenario I took the opportunity to raise awareness of fair use (at best), but I failed to provide coaching. Had I spent some time coaching this instructor on the many considerations necessary to determine fair use, rather than giving him a "black letter" answer, perhaps he would not continue to quote that 30 percent is the rule.

CONCLUSION

In this chapter, we have discussed how copyright education is typically delivered, the necessity for copyright education as an information literacy concept and its overlap with HIPs, and we have also identified some of the situations that librarians encounter which offer opportunities to coach copyright. Librarians are uniquely positioned to coach copyright, and the ACRL Framework provides significant guidance in this regard. Coaching provides the best opportunities for learners to understand and apply copyright and fair use concepts in a real-world, personal way. As faculty and students increasingly explore information in new ways, and simultaneously take on the roles of creators and consumers, understanding the nuances of individual copyright situations will become increasingly important. Coaching takes time, however, and copyright is complex. But real, high-impact learning can occur in information literacy programs that integrate copyright coaching.

NOTES

1. Association of College and Research Libraries, "Framework for Information Literacy for Higher Education," 2016, www.ala.org/acrl/sites/ala.org.acrl/files/content/issues/infolit/Framework_ILHE.pdf.
2. Laura Cruz and Lanise Rosemond, "Coaching Academia: The Integration of Coaching, Educational Development, and the Culture of Higher Education," *Journal on Excellence in College Teaching* 28 (2017): 83–108.
3. Tammy Ravas, "Copyright for Undergraduates: Lessons Learned while Teaching a Semester-Length Online Course," *Journal of Copyright in Education and Librarianship* 1 (2016): 1–10.
4. Gail Clement and Stephanie Brenenson, "Theft of the Mind: An Innovative Approach to Plagiarism and Copyright Education," in *Common Ground at the Nexus of Information Literacy and Scholarly Communication*, ed. Stephanie Davis-Kahl and Merinda Kaye Hensley (Chicago: American Library Association, 2013), 45–74.
5. John Savery and Thomas Duffy, "Problem Based Learning: An Instructional Model and Its Constructivist Framework," *Educational Technology* 35 (1995): 31–38.
6. George D. Kuh, *High-Impact Educational Practices: What They Are, Who Has Access to Them, and Why They Matter* (Association of American Colleges and Universities, 2000).
7. Adam Murray, "Academic Libraries and High-Impact Practices for Student Retention: Library Deans' Perspectives," *portal: Libraries and the Academy* 15 (2015): 471–87.
8. Catherine Riehle and Sharon Weiner, "High-Impact Educational Practices: An Exploration of the Role of Information Literacy," *College & Undergraduate Libraries* 20 (2013): 127–43.
9. Catherine Riehle and Merinda Kaye Hensley, "What Do Undergraduate Students Know about Scholarly Communication? A Mixed Methods Study," *portal: Libraries and the Academy* 17 (2017): 145–78.
10. John Bean, *Engaging Ideas: The Professor's Guide to Integrating Writing, Critical Thinking, and Active Learning in the Classroom*, 2nd ed. (San Francisco: Jossey-Bass, 2011).

LAURA QUILTER

3

Hooking Your Audience on Copyright

ALL OF US WHO TEACH COPYRIGHT HAVE BEEN CONFRONTED with the person who says sheepishly, "I know I *should* know about copyright—I'm probably doing everything wrong and could go to jail!" This rueful self-declaration is really a way of saying, "Copyright has never been important to me, and I don't take it very seriously." But those of us who teach copyright know that it's actually both important and really exciting—we just need to communicate that excitement to our audience.

Once we've overcome that "taking my medicine" attitude, and our audience believes that copyright might be interesting, the real work begins: connecting the audience with the parts of copyright that are most useful to them, and in a way that establishes a structure for long-term retention and growth.

THE PROBLEM(S)

Diverse Audiences

Figuring out how to overcome the "copyright has never been important to me" hurdle requires an audience-centered approach. But librarians face an uncommonly diverse range of audiences that for some varies from day to day.

One thinks of academic librarians as the most likely people to teach copyright, and academic librarians have extremely diverse audiences—from undergraduate students to faculty and every academic rank in between, across all disciplines. Academic librarians also routinely educate administrators and staff, and occasionally members of the public, visiting K–12 students, and others who might interface with or visit the university.

School librarians in K–12 environments are *also* teaching about copyright: first, to students of all ages; second, to fellow educators and teachers within the school or district; and last but not least, to administrators and staff. Copyright education within K–12 environments is particularly common within library and computer programs, but it is not limited to those programs. Indeed, school librarians are often called upon to support and educate students in content creation and accessing third-party content, whether those students are simply accessing content for research or pleasure, or whether they are engaging in creative projects, from music and art to PowerPoint authoring.

Public librarians are perhaps the librarians we least consider as "copyright educators," but in fact there is a tremendous need for copyright education within public libraries. Authors, artists, and innovators, as well as educators and youth, all frequent public libraries and could all benefit from information in a number of related areas: copyright, fair use, public domain content, using Creative Commons content and licensing your own content, licensing, and digital platform publishing on YouTube and Amazon.

Even special libraries offer programming opportunities, since almost all organizations large or specialized enough to support a library are engaging in accessing, using, or producing copyrighted content. And as in academic environments, K–12 schools, and public libraries, very few other entities are both experienced in copyright and poised to offer education about it.

This diversity of audiences constitutes a sort of embarrassment of riches. It's wonderful to have so much opportunity, but how can we actually make effective use of the rich opportunities for programming and education that are present in libraries of all types? More specifically, how can we develop programming in such a (seemingly) esoteric area as copyright, for audiences that range so broadly in discipline, experience, and learning objectives?

Topical Tensions

The second challenge for copyright educators in librarianship is that, frankly, many of our core goals are in tension with one another—and even if they are not in actual tension, they are all too easily perceived to be in tension.

For instance, we want people to care about copyright, so we talk about the more extreme aspects of copyright—copyright terms, statutory damages, outrageous or absurd prosecutions—but this scares people, which is counterproductive. We *want* people to feel empowered and aware of their rights, and yet the very act of teaching them about copyright and raising their awareness of it often engenders guilt or anxiety. We face similar risks when we teach people about the weirder aspects of copyright: internal inconsistencies, politically motivated sections of the statute, provisions so broad they are effectively unenforceable, and unknowable copyright statuses. This level of familiarity tends to breed contempt for copyright among our audiences, which isn't helpful to people in protecting their own rights and managing their own risks. Indeed, the maxim that a little learning is a dangerous thing is as true in copyright as it is in any other discipline. How can we balance passion and knowledge with risk aversion and dangerous contempt?

We also want to politicize people to become aware of both the absurdities and the exploitations within copyright, but we still need people to appreciate the ways they themselves might benefit from or use their rights within copyright. We want them to exercise and advocate for their own rights—within contract negotiations, in using open access and fair use, and in calling for copyright reform. And those rights are their own rights both as users and as creators. In fact, when we talk with someone about their own rights as a user (fair use, de minimis, first sale, etc.), we are simultaneously talking about their rights as a creator—and this necessitates a balance in tone that conveys multiple angles at the same time. How can we balance practical awareness of rights as a user with practical awareness of rights as a creator?

Moreover, as librarians we have our own interests, both as custodians of library collections and as educators of users. As a profession, we support open access, open licensing, and other systems that tend toward more flexible and simpler sharing of information. However, that does not mean that these are always the right answers for individuals in all of their situations. Librarians' interests as activists and policy-makers may not necessarily align with a particular individual's interests in marketing her own work, or aggressively policing it. How can we balance our own advocacy interests with our duties as educators?

Finally, we have the conflicts inherent to any instructional program. We need to tell a coherent story and communicate knowledge, the right knowledge, in the right amounts—not too much, not too little—and still meet the basic pedagogical goals of being interesting and absorbing and having what we teach be retained and, ideally, put into practice.

For all of these reasons, developing the right instructional posture can be challenging when it comes to teaching copyright.

SOLUTIONS
Finding the Hooks and Telling a Story

So librarian copyright educators have two key problems: the diversity within our audiences that require us to constantly shift our content to make it relevant and compelling to our audiences; and the tensions inherent in teaching copyright that sometimes make it challenging to adopt a unitary instructional posture.

The trick is to *find the hooks* for that particular audience, and then pull together a *coherent story* for that audience.

"Finding the hooks" means analyzing the audience in order to understand their particular interests and perspectives, and then figuring out what take-home points will meet those interests. This requires looking at what is distinctive about a particular class of students, as well as remembering what almost all students (copyright laypeople) have in common.

Almost all audiences have two things in common with regard to copyright. First, *everyone*—from the youngest kid able to hold a crayon, to the parents who document every move that kid makes—is a copyright holder. Copyright is literally everywhere, which means that everybody has some skin in the game. They just need to know it. The second thing that most (not all) people have in common is a lack of awareness or concern about copyright. Most people aren't aware that they own copyright, or use copyright, or should care about copyright. When confronted with copyright issues or instruction they will feel a range of diffident emotions, from a vague sense of guilt that they "could go to jail" (often ill-founded, based on activities that are actually wholly lawful), to a vague sense of self-righteousness that they are *not* infringing copyright (also often completely ill-founded, based on deep misunderstandings of what is or is not even copyrighted), to a vague sense of contempt for copyright. A key challenge, therefore, is to find the copyright connections that will get people to care about copyright at all. This can be easy if they already have strong connections with copyrighted works, but it can be more challenging if their connection with copyright is less personal.

Another key challenge is to provide people with something they will actually use—not theory or copyright 101, but copyright that is specifically tailored to their interests. This is not hard, because copyright is so diverse and broad that everyone has a stake in it. Nevertheless, it does require understanding the audience as a first step. Because copyright is fundamentally about *works,* one approach is to look at what works your audience create or use, and why and how. The works they create or use vary according to their discipline. The ways in which they market those works, or use other works— the *how* and *why*—vary according to their career stage and their role in those works' creation.

So almost any audience can be assessed along the matrix in table 3.1, which can help a copyright educator find common approaches to different kinds of audiences.

The second challenge is to tell a coherent story, when we already have so many internal tensions to our story about copyright. Here, the motto "If you can't beat 'em, join 'em" can become your mantra. Copyright instruction can't actually eliminate the internal tensions and contradictions, so instructors must embrace them.

TABLE 3.1

Audience Assessment Matrix: Figuring Out What Will Hook Their Interest

	Type of Works Created or Used	How Used and Why
Discipline: _____		
Career Stages, Publishing Roles, Practitioner Spectrum: _____		

TABLE 3.2

Alternate Approaches to Copyright "Facts"

Simple and Clean (but oversimplified)	Complex and Nuanced (but more accurate)
Copyright is a form of incentivization for creators.	Copyright balances incentives for creators with freedom for users.
Copyright damages can be extraordinarily harsh.	Copyright has extremely harsh penalties, but is also extremely leaky, with robust exceptions and limitations.
Fair use and other limitations protect users of copyrighted works.	Every creator is also a user, and so everyone benefits *both* from copyright and from robust limitations and exceptions.

In copyright, the core of our story is often about nuance and balance; it involves complex perspectives that may not inspire passionate interest and are sometimes hard to convey well. However, it is exactly this complexity that lets us balance the numerous tensions that are otherwise present in copyright education. Ultimately, embracing these tensions helps instructors deal with the ambiguities, and actually helps students, by eliminating the idea that there are simple answers to most copyright questions.

Let's consider the different approaches shown in table 3.2.

The versions on the right are all longer, but they are more accurate in capturing the spirit of copyright law as well as the letter of particular legal doctrines. Just as importantly in the context of a copyright class, this balance helps the instructor and students tell a coherent story, and construct a framework into which the individual facts about creator rights, copyright damages, and fair use will fit.

Finding Hooks across Disciplinary Differences

Disciplinary differences are the first and most obvious distinction in types of audiences. It's critical to assess the audience and tailor your examples, exercises, and the overall content of the session to that audience.

Within academia, we commonly think of academic disciplines in terms of broad categories—arts and humanities, social sciences, sciences, and professional programs. These broad categories, however, disguise enormous variations among the myriad subdisciplines. "Arts and humanities" alone includes every class of copyrighted work in section 102: literary works, dramatic works, musical works, sound recordings, motion pictures and audiovisual works, choreographic works, architectural works, and pictorial, graphic, and sculptural works. Each of these classes of copyrighted works has statutory specifics, doctrinal distinctions, professional norms, and industry practices. And disciplinary genres within these classes further inflect the copyright practices associated with them.

Analyzing an audience's discipline(s)—what works they're producing and using, and how and why they are using them—provides the opportunity to find relevant examples and material. A musical audience will be able to relate to the example of transformative use in music (2 Live Crew's parody of "Pretty Woman" in *Campbell v. Acuff-Rose*), while a literary audience might benefit more from a literature-based example (e.g., Alice Randall's parody of *Gone with the Wind*, in *Suntrust Bank v. Houghton Mifflin Co.*).

Discipline-based analysis also provides a series of ready-made topics and cases of interest. Instructors can develop short lists of cases and doctrines in various academic disciplines, enabling them to easily tailor discussions with their audiences. Here are a few:

Book-based disciplines such as history: Publishers often provide substantial publishing contracts, relative to papers, and every author who publishes a book should understand their contract and be able to negotiate relevant portions of it—including, for example, permissions and the option to rely on fair use. Permissions can be a really significant undertaking for book authors, since a book can include many different excerpts of other works. The same substantive legal issues—are screen captures fair use? Is this work public domain?—will often apply to papers in the same disciplines. The copyrightability of ideas is another key issue, and examples from published books are always popular; for example, *Rowling v. RDR Books* (S.D.N.Y. 2008) delineated what was and was not fair use in a Harry Potter encyclopedia

Science: Scientists and science faculty typically publish research articles, and the images they use are frequently their own creations. Their articles are often submitted through online forms that increasingly incorporate copyright assignment agreements, affording them little or no opportunity to negotiate rights. In this situation, scientists need to understand the contracts they're "signing," and their open-access options.

But scientists and science faculty also publish a variety of secondary and tertiary works, such as review articles, textbooks, and encyclopedia entries. These works often incorporate third-party content and involve negotiable contracts. Scientists in these situations should know about the STM Permissions

Guidelines,[1] which permit the reuse and publication of single figures and images from participating STM members, without payment of fees.

Scientists and social scientists also often raise questions about copyrightability, and whether they can modify existing figures or graphic models. *Ho v. Taflove* (7th Cir. 2011) is an excellent case that discusses the copyrightability of ideas in a science context, and presents a situation that involves faculty in the same department in the university, with graduate students switching labs, that will feel perilously familiar to many scientists.

Arts: Artists are routinely concerned with licensing, employment contracts, and distribution channels—the business side of creative markets. They also focus on questions of copyrightability, fair use, and other limitations.

Within the various art fields, there are numerous specific exceptions. For instance, photographers may be interested in section 120 (which permits the photography of architectural works even if they are copyrighted), as well as in cases relating to works of photography. *Leibovitz v. Paramount Pictures Corp.* (2nd Cir. 1998) is a fun fair-use case involving Annie Leibovitz, a high-profile photographer, and a parodic movie poster for *Naked Gun 33⅓: The Final Insult*. *Harney v. Sony* (1st Cir. 2013), a case about a re-created documentary snapshot, offers an excellent opportunity to touch on copyrightability. The ways that copyright connects to privacy rights and rights of publicity are also a likely topic of interest; *Monge v. Maya Magazines* (9th Cir. 2012) offers a great discussion opportunity. *Drauglis v. Kappa Map* (D.D.C. 2015) is an excellent example of creators misunderstanding their own Creative Commons licensing.

Music: Music, too, is a key concern in many arts fields, ranging from musical recordings on DVDs to video production, to the soundtracks of motion pictures, and to live theatrical performances. The complexities within musical fields—sound recordings as well as musical works, plus connections to dramatic works and choreographic works—offer a lot to discuss in addition to the fundamentals about using copyright or fair use. Across musical genres, there are numerous cases illustrating key points, ranging from fair use in *Campbell v. Acuff-Rose* (parody) and *Lennon v. Premise Media* (SDNY 2008) (fair use to use John Lennon's "Imagine" for effect in a creationist film) to public domain status and record-keeping in the Happy Birthday case (*Good Morning to You Productions v. Warner Chappell Music* (C.D. Cal. 2015).

How and Why: Academic Publishing Roles and Career Stages

Publishing Roles

In academia and in the creative industries, there is a persistent focus on the individual creator: the romantic author scribbling in her garret, the starving musician, the scholar toiling in the library. Even the garage band has a unitary identity as a creator.

In fact, creation involves multiple actors at multiple stages, and in academic production, scholars take on many different roles beyond that of author. Scholars routinely edit special issues of journals or edited volumes, serve on editorial boards at journals or presses, and convene and edit conference proceedings. In each of these capacities, scholars have the opportunity to negotiate their own rights as well as the rights of contributors. The members of an editorial board also negotiate contracts with the publisher and distributors, which is another opportunity for them to engage constructively with copyright around the issues of author and user rights.

Career Stage

Even within a discipline, there are layers. Throughout the various stages of a career, people interact differently with their own work and other people's work, and have different priorities. For instance, senior faculty may feel comfortable arguing for open access because they have achieved tenure, but junior faculty may feel it more important to prioritize publishing in particular journals, and benefit more from a campus-based policy. With regard to copyright, age and professional seniority provide similar advantages, as well as different interests.

Let's consider how librarians work with people in a few different career stages, starting with the youngest and most junior.

Youth: Public and K–12 librarians are often called upon to do instruction sessions for middle and high school students, and even upper elementary students, in which they touch upon copyright as well as plagiarism, citation, information literacy, privacy, security, and other matters—a hodgepodge sometimes called "net safety" or something similar. Young people are sometimes called "digital natives," and they can be quite sophisticated in how they use technology, but as every librarian who works with children and young adults knows, that sophistication doesn't necessarily translate into having the skills to find information, much less understand copyright, fair use, or Creative Commons licensing.[2] Yet this population is learning and using authoring programs to put together PowerPoint presentations and instructional videos, and finding material via search to share and build upon.

The challenge with a class of young people is finding a way to pique the interest of the whole class, when the students may share few common interests or experiences other than their age. Nobody is as bored by an exciting topic as a tween who is passionate about *something else*. For youth, I feel comfortable in amplifying the more dramatic aspects of copyright, and particularly those that might connect with students—the extraordinarily high statutory damages awards in the peer-to-peer downloading cases against Jammie Thomas or Joel Tenenbaum, for instance.

Undergraduates: Working with undergraduates provides some advantages over working with K–12 students: a potential shared interest in the topic of the class, and a likelihood that more of the students have more experiences with searching for other works and creating new works of their own.

Graduate students, post-docs, junior faculty, and early career authors: Graduate students and post-docs are thinking hard about their professional futures, so they have a keen interest in conversations about maintaining their rights and negotiating them, as well as the exploitation and protection of their own works, and the impact advantages of open access. Campus open-access policies most commonly protect faculty, but may be optionally available for use by graduate students and post-docs. Graduate students, post-docs, and junior faculty are also the most publication-hungry, and the most focused on negotiating publishing agreements.

Senior and emeritus faculty and late career authors: Senior faculty and emeritus faculty are much less likely to be interested in negotiating agreements for individual papers, and may feel they already know the drill. However, even late career authors often have things to learn about their publishing and employment agreements. Moreover, late career faculty and authors may be more likely to be offered positions and opportunities that offer new negotiation opportunities with vendors and distributors—such as editing journals, book series, or conferences. Commonly, emeritus faculty and late career authors are interested in securing their legacy, and in considering institutional repository archiving or copyright termination options. The copyright scholar Paul Heald developed a graphic that strikingly captures the relative accessibility of older, out-of-print works based on their copyright status.[3] Showing authors that copyright prevents the discovery of their older works particularly resonates with people who are more senior in their careers, and have a large body of work languishing in the "in copyright but relatively inaccessible" portion of Heald's chart.

Practitioners versus Non-Practitioners

The practitioner/non-practitioner spectrum offers copyright educators another frame through which to reach people, and tailor instruction to what they need.

Practitioners: From the copyright perspective, practitioners are people who are already writing or creating as part of their job; they build on other people's work while they make their own. A "practitioner" can be a musician who covers preexisting works, or who, in writing new work, takes riffs, rhythms, grooves, or quotes from other artists' works. Or think about scientists, who rely on existing protocols, methods, and figures to revise or adapt originals, publish review articles, and teach lab students or classes. Imagine the work of historians, art critics, or communication scholars, all of whom rely on the close analysis of existing works which are often copyrighted, or at least potentially copyrightable.

Practitioners already have a hook: their practical day-to-day experiences with copyrighted works. An instructor just has to pull out the copyright angles, and present these to them. You can develop a myriad of stories that relate to their work in one field or another.

Non-practitioners: Non-practitioners can be trickier, because they don't necessarily have an obvious investment in copyright. This audience might include undergraduate or K–12 students, for example. To reach these audiences, an instructor will need to go the extra mile to find the common experiences that everyone can relate to. For instance, I routinely open classes with general audiences by asking how many of them are copyright owners—and then I amaze them with the knowledge that each of them personally owns thousands or tens of thousands of copyrighted works.

The copyrightability of *everything* can help even non-practitioners connect with copyright via the snapshots on their phone, their e-mails and Facebook posts, and the works of art their children produce by the score. From here, one can connect these quotidian copyrighted works to the problems of historical biographers, family genealogists, and the makers of popular documentary works.

Family, wedding, and school photographs also offer an opportunity to connect people with copyright, via works that are intimately connected to their family but are not (usually) owned by their family. The difficulties that people have run into having cherished family portraits reproduced offer a way to illustrate both the distinction between the ownership of a *copy* and the ownership of a *copyright,* as well as the challenges and injustices of overbroad enforcement, and the need to negotiate or think about rights in these kinds of situations. These conversations often flow naturally into the rights of subjects of works versus the rights of the creators of copyrighted works, as well as privacy and image releases.

Practitioner intermediaries: Somewhere in-between are people who are not the creators or owners of works themselves, but are assigned the often thankless task of clearing rights. Assistants to writers or musicians, editorial assistants at publishing houses, and e-reserves and interlibrary loan staff at libraries all have some practical connection to copyright, but may not have a strong personal interest in copyright as a system. Some staff are particularly interested in how all this works and are eager to take advantage of fair use or other rights. Other staff are just trying to get through a large set of assignments, and (reasonably) want to focus on the bottom line—how to make the process work better.

Sometimes their experiences in rights clearance predispose them to critique the absurdities of copyright: lengthy copyright terms and the lack of a centralized registry of copyright holders, for instance, which can sometimes render ownership hunts and permissions requests utterly fruitless. Other times, however, it might be necessary to look for a hook to pique their interest. The personal element—the copyrighted snapshots on their phone, or the text of their e-mails—can be an effective tool to help them connect to their work with copyright, and construct a larger framework about copyright. Ultimately, it can be most helpful to actually engage intermediate practitioners with the practical substance of their work. If seeking out the rights holders for older materials is tedious and ineffective, then they should definitely know more about how to assess the public domain status of materials, and they should keep Peter Hirtle's indispensable chart nearby.[4] If they are looking for copies of academic works for reserves, then the browser plug-in Unpaywall links to open-access versions of scholarly papers.[5] Editors looking for generic images and stock photos should know how to search for and understand Creative Commons licensed content.

BAG OF TRICKS

Copyright Anecdotes to Shock the Conscience

Sometimes an audience is just difficult to grab. Moral outrage can sometimes do the trick, and tying moral outrage to situations familiar to the student is helpful. This is just a sampling, and copyright educators can readily find additional examples online. TechDirt (http://techdirt.com/) is one reliable source of horrifying abuses and absurdities within copyright, and the more you teach copyright, the more students will share with you their own copyright nightmares.

Academic research and the need for open access: Diego Gomez, a Colombian researcher, faced up to eight years in prison for uploading another scientist's 2006 thesis on Scribd. Although he was found innocent in 2017, the prosecutor in the case planned to appeal.[6] Aaron Swartz, an American researcher and activist, was charged with copyright-related crimes (which could have resulted in many years in prison) for downloading articles from the JSTOR database, potentially for the full-text data mining he had done in previous publications.

The use of scholarly content for teaching: Georgia State University (GSU) and Delhi University have both been sued by academic publishers to stop them from providing access to information. The GSU case is, at the time of writing, still being litigated, ten years on, and instructors were placed on the stand during the trial to discuss their uses of copyrighted works in instruction.

Music file-sharing and outrageous damages: Jammie Thomas and Joel Tenenbaum were both "made an example of" by music industry litigation, with multimillion-dollar judgments for sharing a small number of songs. These examples are *not* useful as "scared straight" anecdotes, to discourage file-sharing or downloading—marquee punishment typically does not have a deterrent effect. However, they are attention-grabbing, and can open up conversations about fairness and economic rationality. It is striking to compare these cases involving large, punitive damage awards in some countries (United States, Mexico, Germany, United Kingdom) with the approaches in

Canada (where fair dealing protects some personal file-sharing)[7] and Spain (where file-sharing is legal).

Copyright takedowns as censorship: In *Online Policy Group v. Diebold, Inc.,* a voting machine company's internal memos were leaked; the memos documented voting machine vulnerabilities, and Diebold tried to prevent this information from being disseminated by sending copyright takedown notices. Although the court found this to be clearly fair use, numerous individuals and institutions suffered the stress of receiving legal notices. Numerous other examples of takedown notices are available at LumenDatabase.org (formerly known as ChillingEffects.org).[8] These examples are helpful in discussing the ease of obtaining copyright, and the potential for misuse; they also open up conversations about fair use and counter-notices.

Negotiating permission requests for all future uses: All too often authors fail to get *enough* permissions when they request permission to use images or other works in their own scholarship. The story of how copyright issues blocked the rebroadcast of *Eyes on the Prize*, a famous television documentary about the Civil Rights Movement, is a useful cautionary tale that will affect many adults.[9] Others may respond to the award-winning 1970s sitcom *WKRP in Cincinnati*, which similarly has not been able to be released on DVD with its original licensed music.[10]

Permissions absurdities: In 2012, Pearson published and sold an art history textbook for $180—with no pictures of art![11] The company cited the difficulties and expense of licensing the art, some of which was actually in the public domain. In addition to licensing and permissions, this anecdote can also usefully open up conversations about open education, public domain, and fair use. Susan Bielstein's excellent *Permissions: A Survival Guide* (2006) offers additional art-related examples.

Negotiating your publishing agreements: In my work, I have seen a number of outrageous copyright situations that would have been alleviated if the authors had negotiated their publishing agreements. In one situation, a junior faculty member's journal publisher sought to charge her $500 to republish a figure from her own paper. In another instance, a graduate student's publication agreement described the paper as a *work for hire* of the publisher, with no rights to include his paper in his dissertation. Finally, another faculty member published a textbook with a publisher, and although he told the editor that he wanted to publish a translation in his native country, he was assured by the editors "not to worry" about his translation rights. When he was ready to publish the translation, with a publisher he had lined up, his original publisher claimed the rights—although they had no plans to translate or publish the work themselves.

Academic publishers targeting faculty authors: Every so often, an academic publisher decides to crack down on the common practice of faculty posting their papers on their personal websites. Elsevier did it in 2013, the American

Society of Civil Engineers did it in 2014, and other publishers and professional societies have done it since. These are excellent teaching moments for faculty, because they afford an opportunity to discuss conventional copyright transfers in publication agreements, as well as open access and the shifts in the academic publishing world. Moreover, they involve counter-notices and the importance of keeping documentation.

Selection of Practically Universal Topics

Copyright educators will find the following topics approachable for many people in different situations.

> *YouTube channel management:* Surprising numbers of people manage their own video channels—everyone from young people who post music covers or instructional videos, to communications or administrative staff who post promotional videos, to instructors and faculty who use YouTube (or Vimeo or similar) for educational purposes.
>
> You can pique someone's interest by discussing the mechanism for taking down (and challenging takedowns) videos or monetizing them; what kinds of background music can get content-flagged or not; and how to respond and challenge a finding of copyright infringement. These topics provide opportunities to discuss, at a minimum, fair use, Creative Commons, the difference between linking and the section 106 rights (reproduction, distribution, public display, etc.), the difference between *law* and *practice* (where platforms and publishers implement their own standards regardless of the law), and potentially many other subjects as well.
>
> *Creative Commons:* Whether people are using others' content or trying to figure out how to disseminate their own content, understanding Creative Commons (CC) licensing is broadly useful. Producers of content of all sorts—amateurs and professionals—need to locate and use openly available content, whether stock photos, clip art, illustrations, or music and sound effects. Instructors can talk about locating CC content in search engines—and this is a particular win for librarians, since it offers the opportunity to connect to advanced searching and facets in other contexts, as well.
>
> The potential licenses within Creative Commons each offer lesson points about copyright. CC-BY requires attribution, which is not otherwise a part of copyright law; this is another point of distinction between plagiarism and copyright, a common confusion. The ND (no derivatives) license provides a back-end opportunity to discuss fair use and the nuances of distinguishing between transformative fair uses and derivative works, such as translations, adaptations to

other media, and abridgements. Noncommercial (NC) and Share-Alike (SA) licensing offer the opportunity to draw connections with open source software, as well as to unpack some of the grey areas inherent in commerciality, such as ad revenue and education. And of course, distributing content via CC affords opportunities to promote a more mindful approach to uploading and sharing content, including the review of default settings (and the concept of "the default").

Contract and licensing negotiation: Understanding how contracts work is generally useful information even outside of copyright work, and thus provides a hook to almost everyone. Almost all adults, and many young people, have signed a lease or a mortgage, taken or given a loan, hired someone for a job or been hired, or purchased or sold something. Each of these actions involves the basic contractual elements that underpin publishing and other transactions around copyrighted works, including, crucially, negotiation. These familiar environments also offer the opportunity to distinguish between exclusive rights and nonexclusive rights, and to delve into the specific aspects of contracting in any particular discipline.

Useful Exercises

Copyright contains such a wealth of detail and stories that it is tempting to fill up a class session with a lecture. But students, whether adult or youth, have greater interest in and retain more material when they are actively engaged in the class.

It's always helpful to have some key questions to start a class and get the mood for discussion flowing. Some extremely useful and very simple questions include:

How many of you are copyright holders? This opens up a conversation about the ubiquity of copyright, which as previously discussed can lead to reflections about the copyright system, or simply help people find a personal connection to copyright. It is also particularly useful for professional creators to understand that they don't have to register to have a copyright. This opens up a conversation about when copyright registration is useful (sometimes) and when copyright notice is useful (almost always). An instructor can also open up conversations about the absurdity of copyright by connecting the ubiquity of copyright to the length of the copyright term. Yes, the snapshots on your phone are copyrighted until seventy years after your death! They will form part of the estate for your great-great-grandchildren.

What questions, problems, or concerns do you have about copyright? This is an excellent open-ended question, and in any group under two dozen or so, you can actually just go around the room and generate a marvelous list of topics to cover. With a little practice, these topics can be grouped into a few common subsets, and an instructor should be prepared beforehand to deal with the common subsets of questions, as well as be responsive to and interact with the audience's immediate concerns. In educational settings, for instance, instructors will commonly raise concerns about the course materials they create, the course materials they have students create, and the third-party materials they use in various ways. There are other ways of breaking it down, but after running this exercise a few times with similar audiences, an instructor will have a feel for the kinds of questions that keep coming up, and what groupings they want to use.

What kinds of things can be "intellectual property" (or copyright)? In business schools or with members of the public, there are often a number of people who are confused about trademark, patent, and copyright. This open-ended question generates lists of trademarks, movies, books, music, inventions, and so on. You can then easily drill down into what is copyrightable and what isn't, how long copyright terms are, and various exceptions and limitations, while constructing a logical framework for the students to understand copyright broadly.

In addition to discussions and lectures, providing exercises for students during longer classes is often very helpful. A few simple exercises include:

A list of hypotheticals: Depending on the topic and audience, hypotheticals can be in the form of a list of problem situations, where the audience spots the problem, or figures out the solution, or both. For instance, you can offer a set of hypotheticals where the students can assess whether to apply fair use or another statutory exception, like subsection 110(1) (classroom performances). Another set of hypotheticals might include brief sketches of works to distribute, or works that a user wishes to use, and then ask for an assessment of Creative Commons licenses.

A hypotheticals list can work in numerous ways; for instance, small group discussion, individual review after discussion, as an icebreaker at the beginning of the session with a revisit during the class, or individual review and then group discussion towards the end of the class. When you generate a list of hypotheticals that connect with your audience, you will often have people coming up to you during breaks to tell you of their real-life experiences with similar situations.

Analyze a contract or a selection of contract clauses: There are a wealth of possible options in contracts, and giving people the opportunity to read through a contract, mark up and strike through its language, and rewrite the language is uniquely empowering. You should use short contracts in order to provide an experience that feels authentic, but doesn't take up too much time. This assignment, too, can be done in table groups; although the reading and markup work best for individuals, a group discussion after a short period can really solidify the exercise.

Role-play a case: For longer classes, or throughout a multi-session course, having students actually read a case, and make arguments about both sides in it, can be an extraordinary experience. Reading legal reasoning helps people see that there are no magic answers—that the law really is about reasoning and analogy. Giving people an authentic experience of legal uncertainty is actually quite helpful because it makes them feel confident about their own legal reasoning.

Arguing the different sides—a sort of mini-moot court—is also enormously fun. Depending on the size of the group, the audience members could do it at individual tables, informally, voting on who "wins," and then reporting back to the group. Alternately, the class can be divided into sides, making and rebutting points.

CONCLUSION

Copyright education is a natural fit for libraries, but it brings a number of challenges—not least among them an enormous diversity of types of students, who often have misconceptions and are uncertain about whether copyright is even important to them. Getting the attention of these students requires a careful analysis of the possible "hooks" in their disciplines, career stages, roles, and practical experiences with copyright. Audience analysis allows copyright educators to come to class with confidence, knowing they can meet the first critical challenge for any educator: engaging the attention and interest of her students.

Once students are invested in the class, copyright educators can help them grapple with the complexities of copyright by presenting them with familiar or engaging scenarios, deploying exercises and topics in ways that resist the tendency to oversimplify and eliminate nuance. Helping students grapple with the nuances and balances within copyright resolves some of the inherent contradictions that lie at the heart of teaching copyright. It also provides students with opportunities to engage copyright in ways that are both reassuring and memorable, whereby they gain useful take-home knowledge and skills and acquire a larger framework on which to continue to build knowledge.

The next time you see those students, they won't be ruefully confessing their imagined copyright sins while failing to realize the real ways their work is affected by copyright. Instead, they will be authentically balancing their own work with copyright concerns, and coming to you to help them tease out additional nuances. That is a copyright education success story.

NOTES

1. STM, "Permissions Guidelines," https://www.stm-assoc.org/copyright-legal -affairs/permissions/permissions-guidelines/.
2. Danah Boyd explores this in *It's Complicated: The Social Lives of Networked Teens* (New Haven, CT: Yale University Press, 2014), available CC-BY-NC-SA 3.0 at www.danah.org/books/ItsComplicated.pdf.
3. Paul Heald, "How Copyright Keeps Works Disappeared," *Journal of Empirical Legal Studies* 11, no. 4 (2014): 829–66, figure 1 (p. 16 of the PDF), available at https://papers.ssrn.com/s013/papers.cfm?abstract_id=2290181.
4. Peter Hirtle, "Copyright Term and the Public Domain in the United States," 2004, last updated 2018, Cornell University Library, https://copyright .cornell.edu/publicdomain.
5. Unpaywall, https://unpaywall.org/.
6. Michael Catanzaro, "Colombian Biologist Cleared of Criminal Charges for Posting Another Scientist's Thesis Online," *Nature,* May 24, 2017, updated June 14, 2017, https://www.nature.com/news/colombian-biologist-cleared -of-criminal-charges-for-posting-another-scientist-s-thesis-online-1.22057.
7. See *BMG Canada Inc. v. John Doe* (2004).
8. For further examples, see Mostafa El Manzalawy, "Bad Reviews: How Companies Abuse the DMCA to Silence Negative Criticism," LumenDatabase blog, July 28, 2017, https://www.lumendatabase.org/blog_entries/797.
9. Democracy Now, "Copyright Issues Block Broadcast of Award-Winning Civil Rights Documentary 'Eyes on the Prize,'" February 8, 2005; transcript and video of news broadcast at https://www.democracynow.org/2005/2/8/ copyright_issues_block_broadcast of award.
10. *Wikipedia*'s article on "WKRP in Cincinnati" has a nice review of the issue, at https://en.wikipedia.org/wiki/WKRP_in_Cincinnati#Music_licensing.
11. Kyle Chayka, "An Art History Book, Minus the Art," HyperAllegic, available at Salon.com, September 19, 2012, https://www.salon.com/2012/09/19/ an_art_history_book_minus_the_art/.

ANNE T. GILLILAND

4

Storytelling and Copyright Education

Romance at short notice was her specialty.
—H.H. Munro ("Saki")[1]

LAW PROFESSORS TRADITIONALLY USE STORIES, THROUGH THE vehicles of case law and hypotheticals, to teach students about the law. Similarly, stories can be an effective way for educators to teach copyright even if they are not training lawyers. Stories help fix facts in our memories, and they are also vital in helping students gain an understanding that goes beyond memory to the legal principles that allow the listener to analyze new dilemmas and situations.

WHY STORIES?

What good are stories? Why do we like them? Stories command a special type of attention from the listener. In general, students read stories faster than other types of text and seem to comprehend information in story form more quickly.[2] The narrative arc of a story draws on our interest in other people, expands that interest, and allows the listener to imagine another person's life. People have used stories for thousands of years to teach social mores, activate empathy, and help us to consider alternative actions and situations. Many of the world's oldest stories, like the epic of Gilgamesh, emphasize the virtues of cooperation and fairness, and we still use certain types of fables and folk tales to illustrate and teach communal virtues and values.[3]

HOW TO USE STORIES

There are (at least) two ways to make stories part of pedagogy. One is the more straightforward method of telling stories to reinforce concepts, increase comprehension, and aid memory. The other is to use the components of story to structure a lecture that keeps the students' interest. Philip Meyer, following the work of the novelist and critic David Lodge and the renowned trial lawyer Anthony Amsterdam, names five components of a story: steady state, trouble, efforts, new state, and conclusion.[4] Daniel Willingham, in a discussion of the effectiveness of pedagogy through storytelling, identifies similar elements, which he calls the "Four Cs": causality, conflict, complications, and character.[5] In either model, the story starts with characters and events in one state or reality. Then the action moves through conflict and problems to resolve in a new status quo.

Regardless of how a teacher incorporates a story, students' minds will react differently to stories as opposed to other modes of communication. Some of this may be attributed to our endless curiosity about other humans, but it also appears to be a response to the way stories are organized. One theory is that the structure of a story provides a chance to solve problems and make connections that are of medium difficulty and so provide maximum enjoyment.[6] Another theory is that even if we have never thought about it consciously, the structure of a story provides a familiar way to learn and remember. We know the story's format from our childhoods, when parents, teachers, and television personalities told us stories that mesmerized us with exciting conflicts or taught us the virtues of sharing and kindness.[7]

Law professors use stories. The traditional format of Anglo-American legal education relies heavily on reading and hearing stories through case law and imaginary scenarios, which are often called hypotheticals or "hypos." The beginning law student reads judicial opinions, which often include a summary of the facts of the case, followed by an exposition of the relevant law, and then by an analysis of how the facts and the law interact to yield a result. Once the facts of the case and its analysis are firmly, or somewhat firmly, fixed in the law student's mind, the professor uses hypotheticals to enlarge and reinforce the lesson. Typically, the professor changes the facts in the scenario and asks if the outcome would now be different. The intent is for students to learn when to generalize, and when not to generalize, based on the concepts they have just learned.

Lawyers also use stories. Often, after a trial, unsuccessful litigants will remark that they failed to tell a story about their client that the jury could believe. An attorney's first meeting with a new client is the process of drawing out the client's story in full. This client interview is akin to a particularly deep and far-ranging reference interview. The lawyer needs to know not only the client's perspective on the incident that sparked the appointment, but also other details, facts, and events that the client might consider to be unimportant or irrelevant.

Part of the lawyer's task at this stage is to absorb and understand the client's story and later rearrange it into a narrative that will yield the best result for the client. I learned this as a first-year law student after my first practice exam in contracts. My professor's most valuable comment to me about the exam was that my analysis should not be bounded by the narrative's structure. Parts of the story may appear in one order in the narrative but may need to be presented and used in a different order for the analysis of the issues. Consequently, spotting and analyzing the issues that a story presents often require picking apart its elements and reassembling them as each issue is considered. What makes narrative sense to the teller is not necessarily the best way to interpret the story's legal meaning.

THE USE OF STORIES IN COPYRIGHT EDUCATION

Many educators who teach about copyright are not training lawyers and are not able to command the time and concentrated focus from students that a law school professor expects. In these situations, storytelling becomes even more important for reinforcing memory and comprehension and then leading students to an understanding of the principles that can be used to analyze new problems. Vivid stories and stories that pertain in some way to the students' lives and careers are particularly effective.

I often begin a class or presentation about copyright with some short stories or anecdotes about copyright that relate to the audience's work or interests or that point to a common paradox. This is especially important when some audience members may not be certain that a presentation about copyright might apply to them. For example, I have begun a presentation about copyright for allied health clinicians with a short anecdote about how my optometrist and I discussed how copyright, as well as patents, might be applicable to the work he does. From that story, I went on to explicitly mention the ways that copyright may be relevant for others who are pursuing careers in allied health disciplines.

I also use these opening anecdotes to foreshadow the ambiguities that come up during many discussions of copyright law. One short story that illustrates this nicely is about a discussion I had on a bus with my fellow riders on our way to work. Their comments about copyright infringement showed the distinction they made between their own file-sharing activity, which they saw as harmless, and the nefarious infringements that other, unknown and unnamed "pirates" commit. This story served as an introduction to the conflict that I used as a thread throughout my presentation, which the audience took up in the discussion that followed. Many people identify with one or both sides of this story, and the parallels to their daily lives are often obvious to them.

One technique that I often use is to add stories to reinforce what is being learned when teaching core copyright concepts, such as the rights holder's bundle of rights or the four factors of fair use. Although it takes only a few minutes to state the basics of these doctrines, the details and application of them are very complex. After this introduction, I begin using case summaries to reinforce these concepts and introduce common variables and nuances. I usually start with an easy example and then work up to harder ones, as we can see in the following three fair use scenarios:

> *Scenario 1:* Students in the radiology department at the medical center have to buy a lot of very expensive textbooks. The books are heavy and aren't always right where the students need them. It would be much cheaper and more convenient if the department would scan the books and put them online. Patient care would probably improve, because information would be at the students' fingertips. The students use all the information in the textbooks at some time or another, so the most useful thing would be to scan every part of all of the books.
>
> Would this plan be fair use? What changes in the facts or circumstances might change your answer?
>
> *Scenario 2:* A professor is going to give a special, one-time lecture on cultural diversity to dental students. She has asked you to scan the introduction to a book on the subject so that she can send it to all the students in the class. The introduction is 5 pages long, and the total book is 367 pages long.
>
> Is this legal? Does a fair use analysis support your conclusion?
>
> *Scenario 3:* You have just written an article about patient care, and in it you use a figure that you have adapted from another article. The adapted figure is shown in figure 4.1.
>
> The original figure is shown in figure 4.2.
>
> In your article, you applied a theory that your colleague had developed and explained in an earlier article. The colleague's article discussed some aspects of patient care, and she illustrated her theory with figure 4.2. In your article, you used figure 4.1 to illustrate your application to a patient care issue in a different, but related field. Figure 4.1 is adapted from figure 4.2 with your colleague's permission, but she no longer owns the copyright in the article she wrote or in the figures that illustrate it, because she signed over her rights in the

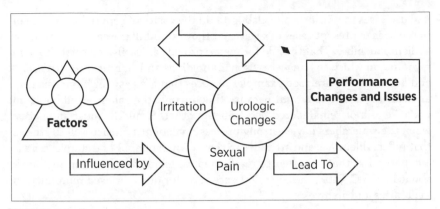

FIGURE 4.1
Scenario 3 Adapted Figure

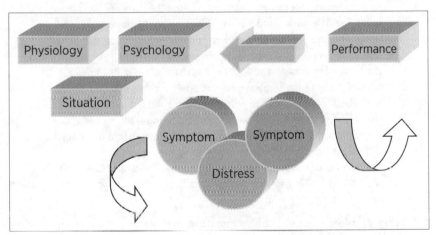

FIGURE 4.2
Scenario 3 Original Figure

publishing contract. You credited your colleague and cited her work in your article, but your publisher says that is not enough. They say that you must contact the publisher of the first article and pay a fee to use your adapted figure. You think that the figures are different enough that you shouldn't have to do anything but give your colleague a credit for the concept and idea. But your publisher says that you have created a derivative work.

Who is correct? What is your conclusion when you do a fair use analysis? Have you learned any other concepts in copyright law that are relevant here?

As I use cases to reinforce and elaborate on the basics of copyright law, one of my goals is to present cases in a way that they can fulfill the same function for audience members that they do for me: to provide an easily accessible hook in my mind on which to hang a case's main holdings and significance. *Kirtsaeng*[8] and *Bobbs Merrill*[9] are good examples of cases that are easy for librarians who are learning about copyright because they involve the sale of used books in one case and of remaindered books in the other. Similarly, most audiences, when their members have a strong professional identity, react well to stories that reflect dilemmas and attitudes in their own domain. For example, here is a hypothetical that I created to teach Medical Library Association members about 17 U.S.C. §108, the copyright exception for unsupervised reproduction in libraries and archives:

> C. is the director of a small hospital library. One day, one of the library clerks that C. supervises points out that someone from the medical records department has been coming in to use the library photocopier every day. The clerk asked him what he was photocopying, and the medical records staff member showed her a recent edition of an expensive anatomy tome. The head of the surgery department had borrowed the book from a friend and told the medical records staff to make a copy of it before the surgeon gave the book back. Now C. is worried, and it seems like whatever she does, someone will get in trouble. Will the person or company that owns the rights to the anatomy book sue the hospital, the library, C. herself, or some other member of the hospital staff for copyright infringement? The surgeon who ordered the photocopying is powerful and known to be hot-tempered, and C. doesn't want to get on his bad side. What is C.'s liability here? How can she protect herself and her library?

This story problem started out as a question that a student asked me during a copyright class. Since then, it has proved a popular and relatable scenario to use in copyright classes for librarians. It illustrates that, with suitable anonymization and changes in context and background, real-life dilemmas and experiences that I have observed or helped solve provide the basis for some of the best copyright stories. Similarly, although I changed the background and subject substantially, the following story started out as a real inquiry from a young employee who was confronting the realities of work made for hire for the first time:

> Katherine is a communications professional who works for a private school. Her job involves a lot of writing, including copy for advertising and promotional materials, website text, and news releases. She is a regularly paid, permanent employee. Katherine feels that she is poorly paid and badly treated in her job, so she gets another, very similar job at a public school where she is much happier. The schools are in

competition often, both in athletics and in their efforts to attract the best students. At her new job, may Katherine reuse some of the copy and text she wrote at the first job?

The students in a class often contribute wonderful stories, usually based on examples from their professional lives. These are often valuable because they highlight questions and problems that are particularly pressing for colleagues or for a cohort at a particular moment in time. For example, I once taught a copyright class to librarians who had all been to another training session that emphasized variations of the CONTU "Rule of Five"[10] for interlibrary loan. As one person asked a question and recounted a story, it became apparent that many others in the class had also had similar experiences and needed answers to similar questions. Most of the class was struggling to understand when they were required to pay reproduction royalties for interlibrary loan transactions.

USING COMPLICATED STORIES

Longer, more complicated stories have their place in copyright education as well. They mimic both the messiness and complications of real-life problems and the complicated issue-spotting questions that law professors include on final exams. These stories normally need to be written down so that the students can follow all of their parts. These are the stories whose narrative order may need to be disrupted during the analysis as a student works through the question in order to fully explore all the issues and their dependencies and ramifications.

The following story details the fictional Dr. Rosebud's film class and film research and the copyright issues that result. I wrote the story for a class on copyright and multimedia for educators and librarians as a final exam question. Kevin Smith was the primary author of the model answer and analysis that are given in the appendix, "Outline of a Model Answer" (see page 87), and it was (and still is) used by students who take the same class.

Dr. Rosebud's Dilemmas in Film Studies

Dr. Everly Rosebud teaches English, film studies, and communications at New Hope Community College at a medium-sized city in the American Midwest. Next semester he is planning a class on film that will include watching films, reading and writing film criticism, and making a short film individually or with a small group. The class has already filled up with 25 students registered. They range in age from 16 to 81.

Dr. Rosebud is planning to use a variety of texts for the class. The primary text is a book called *Cinema: The Mask and the Mirror* that he wrote with his friend and fellow film enthusiast Cameron Hedge. Cameron is an independent filmmaker who works at New Hope Community College as a janitor to make ends meet. The book is not yet published, but the two authors are about to sign a contract with a major publisher.

There are a few things that the authors are not quite sure about. They are hoping that it is okay to reproduce the book and use it for class without registering the copyright. But they are worried about someone else misappropriating their ideas from the book, particularly Dr. Eugene Whiplash, Dr. Rosebud's colleague and rival from Dark Shadows Community College. They are also concerned that somehow New Hope Community College might lay claim to their royalties. Assuming that they are able to keep the royalties, Rosebud and Hedge wonder if there is some legal formula for dividing the money between the two of them.

Then there is the problem of the movie stills reproduced in the book and on the cover. The publisher wants to know if they have received permission from the studios to use the images. Hedge wrote to one film distributor about permission, but never heard back from them. After that, the authors decided that surely the reproductions are covered by fair use; however, their editor at the publishing house seems to think otherwise. Finally, the editor keeps talking about an agreement that Rosebud and Hedge signed. They are pretty sure they signed something, but they can't find a copy of it, and neither one of them remembers what it said.

Dr. Rosebud also wants to use a number of supplementary texts for the class. Some are articles found in journals to which the college subscribes. Others are portions of books that Dr. Rosebud owns himself. He is hoping to have all these readings available electronically, since he knows that many community college students must fit in studying around jobs and family responsibilities. It is often inconvenient for them to come to the library to study.

The students will also watch lots of movies, some in class and some digitized and available through the college's course management system. One of the themes that the class will explore is that of Romeo and Juliet. In some cases, they will watch film clips, and in other cases, they will watch the entire film. Dr. Rosebud would prefer not to take up class time watching entire movies. Also, the college library holds some of these movies on VHS only. But Dr. Rosebud doesn't have a VHS player available in his classroom.

These movies will include:

- *Romeo and Juliet* (1908)
- *Romeo and Juliet* (1911)
- *Romeo and Juliet* (1916; two different and competing films)
- *Romeo and Juliet* (1936, Cukor)
- *Romanoff and Juliet* (1961, Ustinov)

- *West Side Story* (1961)
- *Romeo and Juliet* (1968, Zeffirelli)
- *William Shakespeare's Romeo + Juliet* (1996, Luhrmann)

The students will also make their own films with the Romeo and Juliet theme. They will upload them to the school's intranet, to YouTube, and to their own websites. Some of these films may include:

- Completely original dialogue, using the Romeo and Juliet theme
- Photomontages and stills from the film versions they have watched
- An adaptation of the story, using and changing Shakespeare's words
- New short dramatizations of the story, but using music from *West Side Story* and from Zeffirelli's 1968 film
- Extensive use of the dialogue from *West Side Story,* but in a different setting
- Shakespeare's dialogue, and styled very much like Luhrmann's film but with guns instead of swords and an L.A. setting

Dr. Rosebud is so impressed by some of the films created for this class that he decides to post some of them in future versions of the class so that later students will have examples of really good work.

The model answer and analysis of this story follow below.

APPENDIX

Outline of a Model Answer

Regarding the book that Rosebud and Hedge have written

There certainly *is a copyright* in the book, but we must decide who owns it:

If Rosebud and Hedge signed a copyright transfer agreement, the publisher now owns the rights. If they did not, they hold the rights as joint authors.

- As joint authors, they are entitled to distribute their book to students (or anyone else) any way they wish.
- Because they are joint authors, the law presumes equal shares in the copyright. So the presumptive division of any royalties would be 50/50. Rosebud and Hedge can alter this presumption by a contract between themselves, if they wish.

- Registering the copyright would help them protect the book and entitle them to statutory damages if it is infringed. But registration is not a prerequisite for copyright; that is automatic.

Turning to the use of film stills in the book:

Some may *not be protected by copyright,* if the films are old enough. Rosebud and Hedge could research copyright renewals for films that were released between 1923 and 1963; during those years, renewal after twenty-eight years was required, and an unrenewed film would be in the public domain.

No specific exception in the copyright law seems to address this specific situation, where film stills are reproduced and distributed in a book.

If Rosebud and Hedge found any of the stills in a database, there might be *licensing terms* that they should comply with.

For most of the stills, they should do a *fair use analysis* regarding their use of the stills. In many cases, such use will be fair use, at least for the stills used in the text. The very small amount of an entire film that a still represents is an important aspect of the analysis. The way each still is used—how it is incorporated into the new argument of the book, so that it has new meaning and a new purpose—is the most significant question:

- The lack of response from one distributor is of little consequence; at best it has a marginal impact on the fourth fair use factor, suggesting the absence of a licensing market (and so a lower likelihood of harm).
- The still used on the cover is a different matter, and fair use is less likely. *Permission* should be sought more aggressively for that image.

Issues related to teaching the class

Distribution of course content:

We can presume that the journal articles and book excerpts used in the course are *protected by copyright.*

There is no *specific exception* that helps with the distribution of articles and book excerpts in courses. Remember that the face-to-face classroom exception and the TEACH Act are performance and display exceptions; they do not address reproduction and distribution.

Articles found in databases that the school *licenses* should be linked so that the students, as authorized users, access the articles directly in the database after authenticating themselves.

Articles not available in databases and book excerpts require a *fair use analysis* and some care.

- Book excerpts could be limited to 10 percent or one chapter.
- Items for which fair use is claimed should be limited, and no single source should be relied on too heavily. A single article from a specific journal may well pass muster, but three articles from one issue of a journal would not.

Where the distribution of specific materials does not seem to be a fair use, *permission* can be sought either through a collective rights agency like the Copyright Clearance Center or directly from the publisher.

Students viewing films:

Some of the listed films are likely to be in the *public domain,* primarily due to nonrenewal of the copyright during the period when renewal was required. Research would be needed to determine this, and the difficulty of arriving at a conclusive answer should be taken into account.

Specific exceptions help here:

- In class, (face-to-face) viewing of any of the films is authorized by subsection 110(1).
- Clips that are streamed for online viewing are authorized by subsection 110(2) if all of its requirements are met.

In some cases, the school may have *licensed* a group of films for streaming.

Fair use may apply to streaming the films to students in the class, especially based on the similarity of purpose and market to the situations explicitly authorized by the specific exceptions just mentioned.

Where films are in VHS format, reformatting them into digital versions may be necessary:

If the films are in the *public domain,* there is no difficulty with reformatting them.

For subsection 110(2) (TEACH Act) purposes, reformatting is explicitly permitted by the *specific exception* in section 112 of the copyright law.

There are normally no *licenses* that address the need to reformat films for classroom use.

A *fair use analysis* is needed for many reformatting situations:

- Market harm can be reduced by
- Buying a digital version of a film when one is available.
- Sequestering the VHS version while the digital copy is in use/circulation, so that the school does not benefit from two copies when only one was purchased.

As students make their own films, these issues should be considered

Students will *own a copyright* as soon as their original material is fixed in a tangible medium of expression.

Some of the material they wish to incorporate in their new films may come from films that are in the *public domain.*

- The idea/expression dichotomy permits them to use ideas and discuss topics from even copyrighted films without permission or reliance on fair use. Copyright protects expression, and the copyright in a film version of Romeo and Juliet does not prevent others from using or discussing the idea of ill-fated lovers kept apart due to a family feud, for example.

As students upload their films to social media websites, they should be aware of the *licensing terms* on those sites, which often claim some rights over material that is contributed by users.

There will be a strong *fair use* argument in those cases where they wish to incorporate protected expression if they are careful to make the incorporated work an integral part of their new creation and to use only as much of it as is necessary.

Finally, what should Dr. Rosebud consider when planning to reuse student films as examples for his subsequent students?

There *will be copyrights* in these works, which will be owned by the students who created the films.

Showing the films in a later class may be authorized by *specific exceptions:*

- Subsection 110(1) permits showing the films in a face-to-face teaching setting.
- Subsection 110(2) permits streaming clips of the films in an online class if all of its requirements are met.

A *fair use* argument can be constructed for streaming entire films, as indicated above regarding commercial films.

In order to offer a teaching moment to students, it is probably a good idea to get *permission* from the students for these subsequent uses before the students leave the institution. Although their permission may not be needed in some cases due to specific exceptions or fair use, discussing these plans with students and listening to their reactions is a great chance to initiate a discussion about the positive and negative aspects of copyright in education.

In this specific instance, involving student work, Dr. Rosebud must be aware of the special privacy rights that students have under FERPA, the Family Educational Records Privacy Act, sometimes called "the Buckley amendment." Because of restrictions on the distribution of students' work imposed by FERPA, the permission discussion mentioned above is vital, since written authorization from the students will be needed as a privacy matter, apart from the copyright issue.

CONCLUSION

Stories are far more than frivolous entertainments used to embellish the dry study of the law. They are special ways that we can get and keep other people's attention and teach others and ourselves. It is especially fitting that we should use such a varied, compelling format to teach about copyright law, in our attempt to bring some order to disputes over creative work. Because humans create and because, under the current law, a copyright is formed at the moment of fixation, copyright stories are all around us, waiting to be told and do their part to teach us.

NOTES

1. H.H. Munro ("Saki"), "The Open Window," in *Beasts and Super-Beasts* (London: Bodley Head, 1914), 50–55.
2. Daniel T. Willingham, "Ask the Cognitive Scientist: The Privileged Status of Story," *American Educator* 28, no. 2 (summer 2004): 44.
3. David Robson, "Our Fiction Addiction: Why Humans Need Stories," BBC Culture, May 3, 2018, www.bbc.com/culture/story/20180503-our-fiction-addiction-why-humans-need-stories.
4. Philip Meyer, *Storytelling for Lawyers* (Oxford: Oxford University Press, 2014), 14.
5. Willingham, "Ask the Cognitive Scientist," 43.
6. Willingham, "Ask the Cognitive Scientist," 44.
7. Chris Rideout, "Storytelling, Narrative Rationality, and Legal Persuasion," *Legal Writing* (2008): 68.
8. *Kirtsaeng v. John Wiley & Sons, Inc.*, 568 U.S. 519 (2013).
9. *Bobbs-Merrill Co. v Straus*, 210 U.S. 339 (1908).
10. National Commission on New Technology, *Uses of Copyrighted Works, Final Report* (Washington, DC: Library of Congress, 1979), available at http://digital-law-online.info/CONTU/PDF/Preliminary.pdf.

ANA ENRIQUEZ*

5

Teaching Copyright and Negotiation via Role-Playing

AS A COPYRIGHT LIBRARIAN, I TEACH MEMBERS OF THE UNIversity community about copyright through both formal workshops and informal consultations. In consultations, I often hear from faculty members and other scholars on campus who have questions about scholarly publishing contracts, generally in the form of "Should I sign this?" I cannot give legal advice to members of the university community, so I cannot answer this question. Instead, I have created a new workshop on publishing contracts to help address this need.

ORIGINAL WORKSHOP

I first developed the workshop in summer 2016. As in many workshops I offer, I divided it into two parts. First, I spoke to the participants a bit, using

* At the time of writing, and while developing the workshops, I was a copyright specialist at the University of Michigan Library. I am now the scholarly communications outreach librarian at the Pennsylvania State University Libraries. My thanks go to Jack Bernard, Justin Bonfiglio, Erin Ellis, Mary Francis, Meredith Kahn, Melissa Levine, Jim Ottaviani, Kevin Smith, Rebecca Welzenbach, and Katie Zimmerman, who provided helpful feedback on the workshop materials and this case study.

a slide deck. I talked about the process of publishing a scholarly article and some related copyright concerns. (I did not include a full introduction to copyright, since I regularly offer that in a separate workshop.) Then, after a break for questions, I asked participants to discuss a few hypothetical situations in small groups. I offered this version of the workshop twice, in summer and fall 2016.

I sometimes teach using hypothetical scenarios by simply describing a scenario and then posing a question. For example, I might describe a student's use of copyrighted material and then ask if it is fair use. Or, I might ask whether material licensed under a specific Creative Commons license can be used in a hypothetical instance, or whether copyright covers a hypothetical work. These hypotheticals give the participants an immediate opportunity to practice what they are learning in the workshop. This reinforces the workshop content and helps participants to see its importance.

In a few workshops, including this one on publishing contracts, I take things a step further through role-playing. I lay out a hypothetical scenario, and then I ask the participants to imagine themselves in the scenario and decide what to do. These role-playing exercises have all the benefits of hypotheticals for teaching copyright. In addition, they encourage the participants to think about the practical side of things and what they would actually do in a particular situation.

In my summer and fall 2016 publishing contract workshops, the first role-playing exercise invited participants to imagine themselves on the editorial board of a journal of a fictitious learned society. In this exercise, membership dues and journal revenue (if any) were the society's sole sources of income. The exercise asked the participants to consider what provisions they would want in a publishing contract, as members of the editorial board.

Both times I offered the workshop, I gave the participants some time to consider that scenario, and then I facilitated a group discussion. We talked about how a journal's copyright policies, including an embargo, might impact its bottom line. We also talked about the society's mission—might disseminating the scholarship be more important than increasing revenue? How could the society best accomplish that? How could the society ensure the continued publication of the journal? We talked about societies that had faced financial and logistical challenges in administering their journal and decided to outsource it to a commercial publisher, and what they (and their disciplines) gained and lost as a result. Compared with other discussions of scholarly communications that I have had on university campuses, the discussion in each of these two workshops was much deeper because the participants had put themselves in the position of the editorial board.

Next, we explored the same scenario from the authors' perspectives; that is, those of the contributors to the journal. I asked participants to imagine themselves as first-time authors, and then as authors who had recently been granted tenure. In each case, why were they publishing? What were they looking for in a publication venue? What contractual provisions did they absolutely need? What contractual provisions would be nice to have?

Again, this led to a rich discussion on both occasions. For most participants, envisioning themselves in these roles was quite easy—many of them were in fact first-time authors or tenured faculty. Still, this discussion was richer for their having considered the two author exercises. These exercises complemented the editorial board exercise nicely. The participants were able to see where the two parties' incentives lined up and where they might diverge.

I was quite pleased with how the workshop went in summer and fall 2016. However, after the second iteration, I knew I wanted to expand it. I wanted to make the role-playing exercises more realistic, and I wanted to add some content. The initial framing of the workshop, though it encouraged the participants to think about contract contents and their consequences, did not address negotiating contracts. Yet, it was clear to me that many of the workshop participants could use help in that area. I decided to add to the workshop the basics of the negotiation techniques described in Fisher and Ury's book *Getting to Yes* (*GTY*), the 1981 classic that has become a lingua franca for negotiation.[1]

NEGOTIATION WORKSHOPS

I learned about *GTY* techniques in college and then came back to them several times in law school. Each time, they were taught along with a mock negotiation. Mock negotiations, which are a type of role-playing, are quite popular as a way of teaching these techniques. My experiences with mock negotiations as a student showed me that they are also effective for teaching the substance on which the negotiation is based. I learned family law in part by negotiating a mock divorce settlement, trademark law by negotiating a trademark license, and entertainment law by negotiating an actor's contract. I wanted to give my workshop participants an opportunity to learn copyright law by negotiating a mock publishing contract.

Unlike the simple role-playing exercises from my original workshop, mock negotiations require the participants to have only one role (in this case, author or editor). When most participants in your audience will identify more strongly with one role (in this case, the author), this can seem like a drawback. Some people have to take the role they are not familiar with. However, if you are teaching negotiation using *GTY* tactics, this is actually quite valuable, because it teaches participants to put themselves in the shoes of their negotiation partners, and this is a key element of *GTY*. After the mock negotiation, when participants go on to experience the situation in the real world, they will benefit regardless of whether they find themselves in the role they played in the exercise.

To accommodate a more involved role-playing exercise and inclusion of the basic overview of *GTY* in my slide presentation, I extended the length of my workshop from 60 to 90 minutes and cut some of the copyright material from the slide presentation. I didn't cut the copyright material entirely because I still wanted to provide some framing for the exercise, in order to guard against the spread of copyright misinformation. I then created a new, full-blown role-playing exercise.[2] Instead of asking the participants to imagine what someone in their role would seek, I gave them detailed "role sheets" which defined the roles that participants would step into for the exercise. I also provided a mock contract as the basis for the negotiation.

DESIGNING THE MOCK NEGOTIATIONS

I began by creating an exercise in which an author negotiates the publishing contract for a journal article with a member of the journal's editorial board. I knew there would be interest in a monograph contract exercise as well, but I also suspected the experiences were dissimilar enough that I would not do justice to either one if I attempted to cover them both in a hybrid exercise. I had already experienced this tension in trying to address both formats in the original version of the workshop. Journal articles are used in more disciplines, and their contracts are generally simpler. Since I wanted the workshop to be as discipline-neutral as possible, and I knew it would be difficult to draft a realistic mock contract that was simple enough for a short workshop, I wrote an exercise using a journal article negotiation first. After doing a successful workshop with the journal exercise, I created a monograph one, to be used with a slightly different slide deck.

To design the journal exercise, I began by thinking about the common questions that scholars ask about publishing contracts, as well as the questions I wish they asked more often. I also came up with an initial list of topics that I wanted to cover in the exercise. This tracked closely with the topics covered in my shortened slide deck. For instance, I knew I wanted the exercise to evoke questions about self-archiving, the use of third-party materials, and institutional copyright policies. In the slide deck, I also planned to mention some important resources that would not come up directly in the exercise, such as SHERPA/RoMEO[3] and various authors' addenda.[4]

Next, I looked at several real-life publishing contracts and began writing a mock version that was shorter but still contained the key provisions I wanted to discuss. I also started drafting two role sheets (for an author and an editorial board member). I was careful to consider the interaction between the contract and both of the role sheets, going back and editing each piece of the exercise as necessary. Once I had drafted the exercise, I ran it past colleagues with experience in this area, including some at the University of Michigan

Library's publishing division (which includes the university press). I later repeated the process to create the monograph exercise.

Role sheets are key to mock negotiations. They tell participants what motivates their character. For example, the author role sheets in both exercises begin, "You are an assistant professor at the University. You were hired four years ago and had a preliminary tenure review during your third year. The result of your review was satisfactory, with particular praise for your teaching. You were encouraged to be more aggressive about publishing your research in preparation for your tenure review, which will happen in your sixth year."[5]

Within a mock negotiation, some information is typically provided to both parties. For instance, both parties in these negotiation exercises know that the author's work has been accepted by the journal and the author has been sent the standard contract. However, other information appears only on one party's role sheet. For example, in the journal exercise, the editorial board member has information about the journal's financial situation that the author does not. Also, participants do not know what information the other party knows.

The mock contracts for both negotiations contain simplified versions of common contractual provisions. I wanted the mock contracts to be as much like real contracts as possible, while being concise enough for use during a short workshop. In recent years, there have been efforts to create model publishing contracts that are easier to understand, contain less legalistic language, and are more friendly to authors.[6] These model characteristics are not yet typical, so I tried to avoid implementing them in the mock contracts. Nonetheless, they are relatively easy to understand, because they are short. The mock journal contract is half a page, and the mock monograph contract is two pages long.

FACILITATING THE NEGOTIATION EXERCISES

I have used both exercises several times. Since spring 2017, I have offered five workshops based on the journal article exercise, three based on the monograph exercise, and three hybrid workshops where I used a combined slide deck and the participants chose which exercise to use. Most of these have been open workshops, but I have also offered the workshop for specific groups on the University of Michigan campus, including as a session of the summer First Book Workshop for first- and second-year assistant professors in the humanities and as a dedicated session for the College of Engineering, which is attended mostly by graduate students.

In advance of each workshop, I share the materials as links in a Google Doc and indicate that I will also bring paper copies of them. I try to do this for all of my workshops, to cut down on paper waste and to facilitate accessibility by allowing participants to view materials on their own devices. For these negotiation workshops, I ask participants not to look at the role sheets in advance, in order to preserve the secrecy of the other party's role. This seems to work well: no participant has ever mentioned that she read the role sheets ahead of time and spoiled their secrecy.

At the beginning of the workshop, I work hard to set a friendly tone. Many workshop participants have not done a mock negotiation before, and they can find it intimidating. With relatively small groups, it works well to begin with introductions, asking the participants to share their connections to scholarly publishing. Then, I give my slide deck presentation. I spend roughly the first half of the workshop on the presentation and on answering participants' questions, and the second half on the negotiation. I always reserve a bit of time, usually five to ten minutes, at the end to debrief the exercise as a group.

I keep the presentation as short as I can. If I get the sense that a particular group already knows some of my content, I cut it, either in advance or on the fly. I also tailor the presentation according to participants' questions. However, I find that most audiences need background information in order to benefit fully from the exercise. Without this, enthusiastic role-players will make things up to suit their situation. Unfortunately, excessive creativity can undermine the reality of the exercise.

Publishing norms are highly discipline-specific. On the occasions when I have presented the workshop for an audience in one discipline or set of disciplines, I have tailored the presentation content appropriately. More often, I present this material as an open workshop, where the participants come from many disciplines. In these cases, I give examples of how disciplines' practices vary, I defer to participants' expertise about their own discipline, and I emphasize the tactics and lessons that can be applied in many or all disciplines.

I am also careful during the presentation to tie the negotiation tips back to negotiating publishing contracts. In addition to common examples and stories from *GTY*, which underscore the technique's general usefulness and relevance, I use examples from scholarly publishing. When an aspect of *GTY* would be difficult to implement in a publishing contract negotiation (e.g., tips for in-person or more lengthy negotiations), I acknowledge that and encourage participants to think about how to translate the tactic to their own situation. I also emphasize that understanding and role-playing the negotiation of publishing contracts in depth will be helpful to them even if (as is often the case) the real-life negotiations they encounter later are far more cursory.

Once I have covered the background material, I pass out the exercise in hard copy and direct the participants to the links to digital copies in Google Docs. I characterize the role sheets as "secret facts" and mention that it is up to them to determine how much of their role sheets to share with their partners. This instruction is usually enough to get participants in the right mode quickly. I give a time range for completing the negotiation, thus saving time for debriefing. I direct participants to divide the negotiation time (between reading, strategizing, negotiating, etc.) as they see fit. If needed, I assist in pairing off attendees, and if there is an odd number of participants, I ask two people to role-play as coauthors and negotiate with a single editor.

Once I have given the background presentation and the participants have the materials, I get out of the way. I make it clear that I will answer questions from individuals and negotiation pairs, but I stop talking. The room usually spends at least five minutes in silence as participants review their role sheets and contracts. Then, the partners begin to introduce themselves to each other and talk. When participants have questions, I try to answer them quickly and avoid sustained conversations with any single pair, to ensure there is time for negotiating. I also defer some questions to the debriefing portion, where appropriate.

When we debrief, I ask volunteers to talk about what went well, what went poorly, and whether there were any surprises. This generally yields a very fruitful discussion, better even than the discussions catalyzed by the shorter role-playing exercises in the original workshops. The discussion is particularly rich when participants are willing to share their real-life experiences. This gives the debriefing portion a slightly different flavor each time, depending on who is in the room. (For example, I have been able to draw on the experiences of countless academic authors, several library colleagues from our publishing division, and an attorney from the university general counsel's office.) Having an open-ended debriefing portion also allows me to cover additional substantive content as needed. Often the mock contract gives someone an idea for a new question. For example, we have had excellent discussions of translation rights, reversion rights, and permission searches during this stage.

KEYS TO SUCCESS

Several things contributed to the success of these exercises: making the roles relatable, imposing constraints, making the exercise realistic, carefully calibrating the level of difficulty, and revising the exercises over time.

In a mock negotiation, it helps if the participants can see themselves in the characters they play. The attendees at my workshops typically fill a range of roles at the university: librarians, teaching faculty, researchers, graduate students, and staff. Knowing this, I made the author in both exercises a fourth-year assistant professor. I routinely see early graduate students as well as full professors at these workshops, but it has worked well to make the author roles those of mid-career academics. Participants who are earlier in their careers see their future selves in these roles; participants who are later in their careers see a career stage from their past, but it is not so dissimilar from their current situation that they disengage. I also made the roles in both exercises as discipline-neutral as possible, and I made the partner in the journal exercise an editorial board member of the journal of a learned society, rather than an employee of the publisher, since academics are more likely to have colleagues who are editorial board members, or to be on editorial boards themselves.

Imposing constraints in the role sheets is also important. This helps avert one of the most common problems with a role-playing negotiation: participants, especially those who are naturally agreeable, can give in very easily when nothing real is at stake. Putting constraints in the role sheet and emphasizing the role sheet as a way to get into character ameliorates this. (When role-playing negotiations can be tied to real-world incentives, as in a graded course or a competition, that also diminishes this problem.) In both my exercises, the authors are under heightened pressure to publish due to an upcoming tenure review. Other constraints in the author role sheets include a need to use a few third-party images or figures for which the author has been unable to clear copyright, a university copyright policy that reserves some rights in faculty scholarship, and a desire (framed differently in the two exercises) to make the work available to people who cannot afford paid-for access.

The editor and the editorial board member also have constraints. In the journal article exercise, the editorial board member's role sheet says that the president of the society will have to sign off on any changes to the default contract. The president will review the changes carefully, but she will not typically second-guess the editorial board member. I do this to give the editorial board member room to be creative and authority to negotiate, while underscoring the importance of keeping the learned society's best interests in mind. I also provide details about the society's financial situation, and I impose a realistic requirement from a publisher that handles much of the publishing process on behalf of the society that the society indemnify it. This gives the editorial board member a strong incentive to preserve a clause in the mock contract whereby the author indemnifies the society for breach of warranty.

In the monograph exercise, as in the journal one, the editor is not the final decision-maker. The editor has the authority to negotiate modifications to the contract, but those modifications have to be approved by the director of the press and by its institution's Office of General Counsel. This contributes to the exercise's realism, since academic authors rarely negotiate personally with someone who has complete authority. I also include information about the publication timeline (the proposed deadline in the mock contract has leeway built into it, but receiving the manuscript very late would impact other press projects) and sales data. Finally, I give the press a mission: "Press has a mandate from [its institution] to make scholarly knowledge widely available at low cost, while keeping its budget balanced."[7]

So long as the participants take the role sheets seriously, these constraints prevent them from being overly agreeable.

Constraints are also valuable because they make the exercise realistic. Pressure to publish is real, and a role-playing exercise that neglected it would be inaccurate and would not prepare participants for real negotiations. By making the role-playing exercise realistic, I was able to reinforce participants' understanding of substantive information as well as negotiation techniques. Being realistic meant increasing the complexity and length of the exercise. The three short role-playing questions in the original summer and fall 2016 workshops totaled under 200 words. The mock negotiations are over 1,000 (in the case of the journal exercise) or 1,500 (in the case of the monograph exercise) words. Even so, as mentioned above, both mock contracts are quite short in comparison to the real thing. (The role sheets, too, are simplifications, but participants are able to flesh out the characters from their own experience and typically need little encouragement to do so.)

Setting the level of difficulty of the negotiation is also important. In a mock negotiation, reaching an agreement should be possible, but it should not be easy. If agreement is too easy, participants will not engage deeply with the exercise. If agreement on the face of the exercise is difficult or impossible, the participants may give up, or they may start bending the exercise, which can then make it too easy. To strike the right balance, both sides should have opportunities to make concessions and to stand firm. In the context of GTY's interest-based negotiation technique, this means giving the parties interests that they care about to varying degrees. In the role sheets, some constraints are necessities, while others are preferences.

Finally, I have refined both negotiation exercises, the accompanying slides, and my presentation of the workshop over time, based on feedback from colleagues and workshop participants. For instance, I added a reversion clause to the monograph contract and loosened the future works clause. Both these changes were intended to make the monograph contract more realistic. I have also changed how I structure the slide presentation. In this presentation, I now discuss the negotiation tactics first, followed by the copyright portion. This helps me manage time better, since I generally get fewer questions during that the negotiation portion. It also helps me to engage participants, since the negotiation material is entirely new to many of them.

In my most recent iteration of this workshop, I experimented with assigning roles and sharing the negotiation exercise at the beginning of the workshop, so that participants have a better idea of what to expect and can think about their roles as I go through the slide presentation. This worked well, and I will likely repeat it in the future.

IMPACT OF THE WORKSHOP

Many participants have told me how much they enjoyed these negotiation workshops. As a teacher, I could not ask for a better result. I am certain that this helps participants retain the material, and it also helps me to build relationships with them. They come back to me with questions, they refer their colleagues, and they help to publicize future workshops.

I have had a few participants leave the workshops early, either shortly after I went over the role-playing format or after the slide presentation, just before the role-playing exercise. I attribute this in part to the enjoyable nature of role-playing exercises and their rarity in academic library workshops. These exercises can seem like a frivolity, rather than a serious teaching tool. I have heard from several participants that they felt a bit silly at the outset of the role-playing exercises and were surprised in the end at how rewarding they were. I now mention this at the beginning of each workshop. I also tell participants that role-playing exercises are a common tool for teaching negotiation, and that I learned negotiation through role-playing. These measures seem to have made a difference. In addition, addressing this issue is one reason why I experimented with introducing the role-playing materials earlier in the workshop, so participants would see the connection between the presentation and the role-playing exercise better.

I have seen high demand for this workshop, both in registrations for open workshops and in requests for customized private ones. Since former participants are happy to help with publicity, I reach increasingly broad audiences. In addition to drawing in more participants for the workshops themselves, this has led to more participants in other workshops and to a greater number of contract-related consultations (both with workshop participants and with others).

My consultations with people who have participated in these workshops are a joy. The background provided by the workshop enables them to ask useful questions, both of me and of their publisher. Although I do not give them legal advice, they get what they need to make their own decisions. What is more, these consultations are an excellent source of feedback on the workshop materials, feedback which I then incorporate into future versions of the workshop. My initial goal of helping patrons with publishing contracts without giving them legal advice has definitely been met.

An unexpected, but very encouraging, piece of feedback was that the workshops cause participants to see that there are real people on the other side of these negotiations. I have heard several variations on this theme. For some participants, the revelation is that their editor has needs and vulnerabilities of her own. This makes the process less scary for the participants as authors, and it encourages them to stand up for what they want. For others, realizing that there is a real person reading their e-mails spurs them to politeness. That this has been a revelation for so many participants shows how bad things have gotten—indeed, many publishers even cultivate an impersonal attitude by situating the publishing agreement within the submission form or presenting it to the author with only a checkbox, with no opportunity for discussion or negotiation. However, *GTY* is heartening here. Politeness makes a difference during a negotiation, and so does standing up for yourself.

Given the success of these mock negotiations, I am looking for other opportunities to increase my use of role-playing in teaching copyright. Next up is the expansion of a set of basic role-playing exercises that teach participants to teach others about copyright. I look forward to seeing how the benefits of role-playing play out in that context.

NOTES

1. Roger Fisher, William Ury, and Bruce Patton, *Getting to Yes: Negotiating Agreement without Giving In,* 3rd ed. (New York: Penguin Books, 2011).
2. Ana Enriquez, "Negotiation Exercises for Journal Article Publishing Contracts and Scholarly Monograph Publishing Contracts," last modified May 2018, http://hdl.handle.net/2027.42/143861.
3. SHERPA/RoMEO is a database of the copyright policies of scholarly journals. See SHERPA/RoMEO, www.sherpa.ac.uk/romeo/index.php.
4. See University of Michigan Library, "University of Michigan Author's Addenda," https://www.lib.umich.edu/copyright/authors-addendum; Big Ten Academic Alliance, "The Big Ten Academic Alliance Statement on Publishing Agreements," www.btaa.org/docs/default-source/library/authorsrights.pdf; and SPARC, "Addendum to Publication Agreement," https://sparcopen.org/wp-content/uploads/2016/01/Access-Reuse_Addendum.pdf.
5. Enriquez, "Negotiation Exercises," 3, 8.
6. For an example of a more author-friendly publication contract, see Lisa Macklin et al., "Model Publishing Contract for Digital Scholarship," http://dx.doi.org/10.3998/2027.42/138828.
7. Enriquez, "Negotiation Exercises," 9.

MERINDA KAYE HENSLEY

6

Undergraduate Research Journals as Pedagogy

UNDERGRADUATE RESEARCHERS AS CONTENT CREATORS HAVE two main things to learn about copyright: how to abide by the guidelines for use in creating their own work, and determining how they want their scholarly work to be disseminated and, in turn, used. Both of these critical understandings influence each other, and the student's experience within an undergraduate research program and its requirements could potentially shape the way our society understands and tries to update intellectual property rights in the future. Furthermore, the impact of global exposure to undergraduate scholarly work on the open web has myriad implications for students' growth along the information literacy continuum, most importantly for their understanding of advanced scholarly communication concepts such as copyright and the issues related to authors' rights.

In an overview of high-impact educational practices, George Kuh outlines the goals of undergraduate research as "involv[ing] students with actively contested questions, empirical observation, cutting-edge technologies, and the sense of excitement that comes from working to answer important questions."[1] Undergraduate research often requires students to engage the scholarly community by sharing a summative "publication," such as an article in an undergraduate research journal. According to a statement released in 2005 by the Council on Undergraduate Research (CUR) and the National Conferences on Undergraduate Research (NCUR), undergraduate research is a four-step process:

1. The identification of and acquisition of a disciplinary or interdisciplinary methodology
2. The setting out of a concrete investigative problem
3. The carrying out of the actual project
4. And finally, the dispersing/sharing of a new scholar's discoveries with his or her peers—a step traditionally missing in most undergraduate educational programs (NCUR).[2]

The expectation for sharing student work is growing rapidly within the curriculum across all disciplines, and step 4 in the list above brings students full circle in the scholarly communication process. Students as scholars are sharing their ideas and results through typical academic channels—poster presentations, undergraduate theses and capstone projects, panel presentations, theatrical performances, multimedia projects, coauthored manuscripts with faculty mentors in professional journals, and—the focus of this chapter—publications in campus-led undergraduate research journals. It is worth noting that undergraduate research journals are increasingly being indexed in disciplinary databases, local catalogs, and search engines such as Google Scholar. Student work is also being submitted to and archived in institutional and disciplinary repositories. It should come as no surprise, then, that student work is progressively being cited in refereed journals, dissertations, and other theses.[3]

Academic institutions are investing in the creation of undergraduate research journals in order to promulgate the in-depth and often impactful work produced by formal undergraduate research programs. When it comes to writing an article for an undergraduate research journal, students are both consumers and producers of knowledge, and so they are responsible for both managing copyright issues as they construct (and reconstruct) their writing as well as managing their rights as published authors, whether they understand the ramifications of copyright or not. The opportunity to prepare a manuscript for publication in an undergraduate research journal is parallel to the professional experience that a tenure-track faculty member undergoes, including the submission process, peer review, and copyediting. Therefore, how student journals are set up is essential for establishing a beginner's understanding of the implications for disseminating scholarly work. It will also influence students in one of three ways. (1) Students are pulled into the existing status quo of signing away their rights and only later realize the implications of that decision and their ability to manage their work (e.g., publish the same results in a professional journal or share their work openly). (2) Students hold their copyrights, but do not realize the implications of this because there is no statement to guide them. And (3) students retain some or all of their copyrights, but may or may not grasp their corresponding responsibilities as copyright owners. Each of these scenarios presents educators and librarians with a teachable moment to challenge students' assumptions about what it means to share their journal article online—assumptions which are primarily based on their experiences as consumers and content creators on social media.[4]

This chapter will discuss opportunities for librarians to engage with students who are publishing in undergraduate research journals and, in particular, influence copyright statements and author's agreements during the development of those journals. We will also discuss how sharing undergraduate students' work online necessitates teaching students about intellectual property rights, and we will describe the campus libraries' collaboration with the Office of Undergraduate Research at the University of Illinois at Urbana-Champaign.

SETTING THE STAGE FOR TEACHING UNDERGRADUATE RESEARCHERS ABOUT INTELLECTUAL PROPERTY RIGHTS

Not surprisingly, students expect to be able to share their scholarly output on their own websites and social media platforms (e.g., YouTube for performances and multimedia projects, or providing links from an Instagram account and Snapchat stories) and this, for better or worse, influences their views on sharing their creative output. Nevertheless, common misunderstandings about the legal parameters of creating and sharing can confuse these students' understanding of complex intellectual property issues. For example, when Chris Hadfield performed David Bowie's "Space Oddity" in the International Space Station, he sparked a conversation that encouraged us to envision a world where everything is connected and may even be "subject to terrestrial intellectual-property regimes."[5] Fortunately, Hadfield had obtained permission to record and distribute his rendition of the song on YouTube, but without explaining this background detail to his audience, students may be left with the assumption that this type of sharing does not incur any consequences. Ownership issues are tricky, and students may apply their (mis) understandings of sharing on social media to their ability to share their creative scholarly output online.

Myths of intellectual property rights abound, as demonstrated by the list of "Common Copyright Myths" compiled by the Case Western Reserve University Library. Several of the myths listed there may be familiar to students: "Educational use means I always have fair use for anything I need to use," "It's already on the Web, so it's public domain," and "I can't be sued for much money, anyhow."[6] Students may have a fleeting recollection of fair use principles due to their consumption of video, but they don't necessarily connect legal parameters to their own responsibilities, especially when their favorite YouTubers (novice and prolific posters alike) express frustration at what seem to be, on the surface, abusive takedown processes.

A recent study of undergraduate researchers from Illinois and Purdue demonstrates students' confusion about who owns the work they have created as part of their educational experience. For example, interviewees expressed confusion regarding the preconceived notion that "the author always has the rights to copy his/her own work," and many of them were willing to allow the university take ownership of their work if it meant their conclusions would be shared at the annual undergraduate research symposium. As a second example, students working in a lab environment held problematic beliefs regarding who owned the data they collected, in part because they expressed distance from the research process as a whole. These examples expose students' tendencies to sometimes take their understanding of ownership too far and sometimes not far enough.

There are a variety of teachable moments experienced by student researchers that offer unique challenges and opportunities for understanding intellectual property rights. For example, when two STEM students are presenting a poster on coauthored research in a lab, it is their responsibility to consult with mentor(s) to make sure that the data/images/graphics used are not only accurate, but also that they have secured appropriate permissions and provided proper attributions for them. In addition, as creators of that same research poster, students may choose to contribute to the larger conversation in their field by submitting the digital file and corresponding metadata to an institutional repository. There are implications of global exposure that arise when student work is shared beyond the local level, complications that could hold the students legally responsible for their decisions. These increased obligations to an ethical scholarly process translate to a corresponding awareness of the need to teach undergraduates about their roles and responsibilities within the intellectual property environment.

In fall 2017, the University of Southern California designed an undergraduate course to address the "IP education gap." This course, "The Entrepreneur's Guide to Intellectual Property," is a "first-of-its-kind course for general (non-law) undergraduates on the basic workings of patents, copyrights, trademarks, and trade secrets in social and economic life."[7] The text created for the curriculum was David Kline et al.'s book *The Intangible Advantage: Understanding Intellectual Property in the New Economy* (2016), the first-ever intellectual property textbook geared toward undergraduate students.[8] The course is complemented by a series of three-minute videos that explain patent, trademark, and copyright issues related to the business world.[9] This is an example of how to design a course addressing the nature of intellectual property rights from a disciplinary perspective, in this case business and entrepreneurism.

However, until intellectual property rights education becomes a mandatory part of the undergraduate curriculum, there is a strong argument to be made for the librarian's role in prioritizing outreach and disciplinary partnerships in order to teach students about a wide variety of issues related to intellectual property.[10]

BENCHMARKING INTELLECTUAL PROPERTY RIGHTS AND THE UNDERGRADUATE RESEARCH JOURNAL

In 2014–15, Heidi Johnson and I performed a research study to benchmark our collective understanding of how many undergraduate research journals were being published on a regular basis, as well as to compare the intellectual property rights language used by those journals with that used by professional academic journals.[11] We established a near-comprehensive index of approximately 800 journals and defined a sample pool of 278 titles to canvas for qualitative data elements regarding each journal's setup and management. We wanted to use the resulting data about the peer review process, library involvement, and journal professionalization to draft a set of guiding principles that could be used by students and faculty mentors to assist in devising (or reenvisioning) these journals' setup. The complete index along with the qualitative data is published in the Illinois Data Bank.[12]

Two of the qualitative characteristics we searched for was whether or not each journal provided a copyright statement, and if so, did students keep or sign away all or part of their rights? We concede that in looking at the final data, we cannot necessarily assume that the faculty mentors and students who set up each journal had not considered aspects of authors' rights; we know only that the journal websites did not include that information. However, we suspect it is safe to assume that faculty members apply their experience as authors, peer reviewers, editors, and as disciplinary readers to assist students with the setup of undergraduate research journals. Ultimately, we were curious to learn if student journals would reflect a similar environment as professional journals, with many of them asking students to sign over their copy rights pro forma.

With the advent of open access publishing, the movement for authors to retain their copyrights has gained momentum. Oftentimes, open access is viewed as going hand-in-hand with authors retaining their copyrights, although in our study the results were not that simple. In our sample of 278 journals, almost 90 percent of the titles were open access ($n = 245$), leaving only a few as either a print-only publication or a subscription-based publication. Whether the journal was open access or not, 122 journals (44 percent) included some sort of copyright statement, and of these, 25 percent ($n = 70$)

indicated that students retained their copyright, 16 percent (n = 43) indicated that students signed over their copyright, and 3 percent (n = 9) had a copyright statement giving students some rights, but not exclusive rights to their own work. Only one journal, *Paideia: International Philosophical Journal,* published in Germany, licensed its works with a Creative Commons license. Over half of the journals surveyed contained no public information regarding the students' copyrights. Similarly, author agreements were rarely found on the journal websites, but further research is needed to determine whether or not there is a trend of formalizing the process behind the scenes.

Librarians can use this data to develop outreach and communication strategies to assist faculty mentors and students in the professionalization of undergraduate research journals by initiating discussion on intellectual property rights and by making a point to provide sample language options of copyright statements and author's agreements. Hopefully, librarians will be invited to be involved at the planning stage for a new undergraduate research journal, but librarians can also reach out to existing journals under the guise of journal professionalization. The benefits of librarian involvement for students and the faculty mentors who manage undergraduate research journals are twofold: the librarian's input gives credibility to increasingly important academic publications, and the librarian's expertise with the ACRL "Framework for Information Literacy for Higher Education" (the Framework) and its frame "Information Has Value" can translate to meaningful one-on-one interactions and effective information literacy instruction.[13]

THE LIBRARIAN'S ROLE IN DEVELOPING UNDERGRADUATE RESEARCH JOURNAL DOCUMENTATION

As seen in the Library Publishing Coalition's "Directory," campus libraries continue to expand their publishing initiatives, and many include student journals within their current portfolio.[14] The outreach and instructional services that support the publication processes of scholarly society journals, open educational resources, open access monographs, and digital scholarship projects (e.g., Scalar and Omeka) could be adapted for undergraduate research journals.[15] For example, many libraries are already providing guidance on setting up a journal's structure (e.g., editorial boards and submission guidelines), workflow setup, publication templates, graphic design, copyediting, and marketing. In addition, Fagan and Willey point out that "as more faculty come to recognize student research as part of the institution's scholarly output, librarians can be ready to show how student research can be included in local scholarly spaces like institutional repositories and in abstracts and indexes."[16] Librarians are also working to professionalize student journals by making sure that undergraduate research is accessible outside the institution through the assignment of ISSN numbers and digital object identifiers (DOIs) and by indexing titles in online catalogs such as WorldCat, *Ulrich's Periodical Directory*, and the Directory of Open Access Journals (DOAJ).[17] In addition to making undergraduate scholarly work accessible, there is a need to provide structure around the intellectual property issues faced by students, mirroring the processes that faculty face in the scholarly communication cycle.

There is little understanding of undergraduate research journals as a community within the higher education or information sciences literature. Consequently, there are few resources that provide guidance on a community-wide set of best practices to follow when setting up an undergraduate research journal. In 2012, the CUR published a guide, *How to Start an Undergraduate Research Journal*, with chapter 2 providing a smattering of advice on copyright issues.[18] The book's author, Alexis Hart, depicts copyright as a "potential stumbling block" when it comes to the creation and sustainability of an undergraduate research journal. Intellectual property rights statements, possibly written in laymen's language, could help students acquire a more complete understanding of how to use previously published work in their current creative activities. Proper guidance could also help students distinguish between proper attribution and plagiarism and how that situation differs from fair use and the need to seek permission when including a graph or chart within their manuscript. Hart also points out that restrictive author's agreements can discourage submissions to undergraduate research journals because students and/or faculty mentors may want to publish their findings in a professional disciplinary journal, and an undergraduate research article may be deemed as "previously published" and rejected for that reason. An author's rights agreement should encourage students to think about what they may want to do in the future with their work and to consult with their faculty mentors or reach out to a disciplinary journal to see if it considers an undergraduate journal publication to be previously published work, even if the author retains his or her rights. To mark the importance of crafting articulate intellectual property language that students can understand, the author recommends that the editorial board leadership of the undergraduate research journal contact their local office of general counsel to make sure they are in concert with institution-specific requirements.

THE PEDAGOGY OF BASIC COPYRIGHT AND AUTHOR'S RIGHTS IN UNDERGRADUATE RESEARCH JOURNALS

As undergraduate research writers, students are prepared to engage information privilege in an authentic, experiential learning environment.[19] Information privilege is one of the dispositions outlined in the ACRL's Framework, and is defined by understanding the difference between navigating from behind the paywall where students have access to a plethora of paid library resources in comparison to the realization that most of the public does not have the same access.[20] Hare and Evanson tie this concept to undergraduate publishing efforts: information privilege is the "core tenet . . . that undergraduate students' work is worth sharing openly, if they so choose."[21] There are a growing number of librarians who are teaching information privilege as applied to publishing, and the technique is best described by Char Booth's pedagogical strategy, which "encourage[es] appropriate attribution and permissions practices, and exhort[s] students to understand their own voices as valuable contributions to an ongoing interdisciplinary discourse."[22] Furthermore, experiential learning states that as students go through a concrete learning experience (submitting their manuscript to an undergraduate research journal) with active experimentation (including working with a librarian), the subsequent reflective observation elevates their understanding by modeling an existing abstract concept (e.g., previous "publishing" experience through social media).[23]

Students' ability to learn is heightened when their own scholarly work depends on it. First and foremost, when students make purposeful and informed decisions to share their scholarly work openly, they directly influence if and how future researchers can build off the resulting research, thereby fulfilling the promise of the scholarly communication cycle. Second, when students translate their publication into a citation, they can better understand the importance of seeking permission to reuse content. Their decisions as authors and copyright holders also influence the possible commodification of their "publication" by companies looking for an easy profit, and counter the perception that information is free.[24] Third, the impact of combining the Framework and information privilege with experiential learning could prepare and empower students to effect change down the road in reconstructing intellectual property laws for sharing online because they can see how those laws impact their work.

CASE STUDY

University of Illinois at Urbana-Champaign

The Office of Undergraduate Research at the University of Illinois Urbana–Champaign administers a Research Certificate Program that offers participating students a credential they can share with prospective employers and graduate schools.[25] To qualify for the certificate, students must give two in-person presentations of original research at a conference or symposium, complete nine hours of coursework related to undergraduate research, and attend one campus workshop or professional research presentation and submit a corresponding one-page summary. The following is a lesson plan for a newly developed workshop on copyright and author's rights for students who are preparing to publish for the first time in an undergraduate research journal.

WORKSHOP TITLE: Everything You Need to Know about Publishing in an Undergraduate Research Journal

TIME: 90 minutes

DESCRIPTION: Are you getting ready to publish in an undergraduate research journal? Come to this session taught by the University Library to learn about your responsibilities as an author: how to apply fair use so that you can confidently and properly use previously published graphs, charts, and much more in your article; what you need to know about your copy rights, and how to read an author's agreement which is required when you publish in an undergraduate research journal at Illinois; and consider what the impact will be of your article on future research.[26]

LEARNING OUTCOMES (Put on a slide before class):

1. **Production:** Students will review three case studies from undergraduate research publishing in order to practice applying the elements of fair use as evidenced by completing a worksheet with two new scenarios.

2. **Dissemination:** Students will compare their previous experience with sharing content online with an example of a copyright notice in order to prepare for upcoming publication, as evidenced by the students' answers to a comprehension check.

3. **Management:** Students will investigate two student publications in order to uncover the impact of that work as evidenced by the quality of a group discussion.

   Anticipatory set: The workshop begins with three questions to generate conversation and informally assess the students' prior knowledge (10 minutes).[27]

   Question 1 (production): True or False with https://www.polleverywhere .com/. (1) Educational use means I always have fair use for anything I need to use in my final paper/video/digital project. (2) The source is old; I can't find the owner, so it's okay just to use it. (3) The source is already on the Web, so it's public domain. (4) Copyright is the same online as it is in class. (5) Nobody is watching academic use.[28] Briefly discuss the results of this question with students, without going in-depth on the principles of fair use (this will be covered in the next section).

   Question 2 (dissemination): By a show of hands—how many students have shared content online in a space such as YouTube or Twitter? When you share online, do you read the terms of service first to make sure you're not violating them? (Provide a brief overview of the Hadfield example as explained earlier.)[29] Remind the students to prepare ahead of time to decide how they want their work shared and used by others, and to read the terms of service before they post in order to understand their responsibilities within the agreement.

Question 3 (management): How much would you be willing to pay to read an article that is directly related to your research? Share a screenshot of a vendor page requiring payment for an article. Define "open" versus "closed" access and include some data about the economics of purchasing academic journals at the University of Illinois. Remind the students: if the log-in is through the library, they have access to research through their tuition dollars, but when they graduate they will not, and will be asked for payment.

Tell a Story (3–5 minutes): "Students are proving they are savvier than adults in understanding intellectual property rights. In 2015, the Lewisville Independent School District in Texas was sued by a student when they insisted students sign a 'work for hire' agreement that gave the district sole ownership over photos taken as part of a yearbook class. The student, Anthony Mazur, (who gained national attention by using the hashtag #IAmAnthony, a play-off of #JeSuisCharlie), was vindicated when the administration agreed to stop requiring that all students sign the agreement, now and in the future."[30] This situation should resonate with students and clarify how and when copyright is assigned—as soon as a work is created, and no registration is necessary.

1. PRODUCTION: Challenging Students' Assumptions

PEDAGOGY: Kevin Seeber suggests that we move away from the pedagogy of punishment when teaching students about the risks of plagiarism and instead take a critical approach to citation instruction as the "means to support their ideas and situate themselves among other scholars."[31] Similarly, this workshop models fair use analysis by not emphasizing the punishment students could face for "not following the rules"; instead, we empower them to make their own reasoned decisions. The example scenarios directly relate to manuscripts being prepared for undergraduate research journals.

Discussion (15 minutes): Very briefly, discuss the basic principles of fair use, and hand out the "Fair Use Fundamentals" flyer and the fair use analysis worksheet.[32] Students are presented with three case studies, and together they should review and consider the four elements of fair use. The students are encouraged to document and archive their analyses using the worksheet as an example.[33] Each scenario is reflective of a common situation that undergraduate students may face as they write their manuscripts for an undergraduate research journal. Scenarios: (1) Can I use this chart/table/visualization in my manuscript? (2) I would like to use a map that was printed by the government in my manuscript. Is that okay?

(3) I am planning to use a table that was created by my faculty mentor and was published in one of her first articles—can I just ask her for permission to use it? You should encourage the students to reach out to a librarian when they find themselves in a situation where they would like to reuse content.

Comprehension check (3 minutes): Ask the students to consider an additional copyright myth, "E-mails aren't copyrightable, pass it along!" How does this fit into what we've discussed so far?

Activity (5 minutes): Part 1—Apply the principles of fair use to two scenarios and then fill out the worksheet. Scenario 1: I use primary sources as part of my research, and I would like to reprint a copy of a 1600s personal letter from the archives in my article. Who do I need to ask for permission to include it in my manuscript? Scenario 2: I published my first article as a coauthor with a graduate assistant mentor. Can I post the PDF to my online portfolio? Part 2—Hand out business cards and suggest students put the librarian's contact information in their phone contacts for when they are ready to ask a librarian for help with fair use determinations and/or requesting permission to use previously created materials.

2. DISSEMINATION: Students Own Their Scholarly Work Unless They Choose to Sign Their Rights Away

PEDAGOGY: Students have been solving their issues related to copyright since they were old enough to create content to be posted on a social media platform. This approach is called "single loop learning" because students have most likely relied on their understanding of sharing based on what they see their peers doing online, and they have not yet experienced consequences for their actions. "Double loop learning" produces new actions by aligning the learner's theory-in-use with the new meaning, in this case an understanding of author's rights.[34]

Discussion (10 minutes): We suggest that students ask themselves several questions when they are thinking about publishing their creative output: What do you want to do in the future with your work? Have you consulted with your faculty mentor to get their advice on where/when to publish? Are you considering publishing the same work in a professional journal in the future? We emphasize that copyright is a bundle of rights, not rules. We also define Creative Commons licensing as an option when sharing on the open web in lieu of formal publication.[35]

Comprehension check (3 minutes): Ask the students: Do you think you have signed away your rights in the past? Ask the students to provide examples from common social media platforms, and comment as needed.

Activity (10 minutes): Discuss an author's rights agreement example from the University of Illinois journal *Re:Search: The Undergraduate Literary Criticism Journal at the University of Illinois.*[36] Discuss the following: What does it mean to own your work? What does it mean for you as an author to "grant to the University the non-exclusive right to reproduce, translate" your article? Under what type of scenario would the library translate your work for the purposes of "security, back-up, and preservation"? How do you prove that you have secured permission to reproduce a graph/chart/table/graphic for your article? What rights do you have as copyright owner to your work after you have submitted it to a journal published by the library?

3. Management: Making an Impact

PEDAGOGY: An example of constructivist learning theory in action is the case study. Case studies provide example situations that are an essential touch point for students to see themselves in a newly constructed narrative and imagine how they might make the same or different choices.[37]

Discussion (10 minutes): Demonstrate the value of open-access work by sharing two case studies of student work from the University of Illinois: one from the journal *Re:Search,* and one from the University of Illinois' institutional repository, IDEALS. Talk about the value of citation counts and how these scholarly works now fit into the cycle of scholarly communication. What does "closed access" mean? Why would a scholar choose to publish in a "closed" (i.e., non-open access) journal? Give an example of database access versus open access. How would a scholar outside the United States read a published article? Ask students about their opinion of open access. If students want to know more, they can be part of the student movement through the Scholarly Publishing and Academic Resources Coalition (SPARC).[38]

Comprehension check (3 minutes): Test the advocacy role of students by asking, "What does it mean for a scholar to get x-amount of downloads for their article in an institutional repository?

Activity (5 minutes): Provide time for students to peruse the "Undergraduate Research" community section of the IDEALS website.[39]

4. Final Assessment

Ask the students to reflect on their learning experience by administering a one-minute paper: "In consideration of what you have learned today regarding your role in determining fair use, your responsibilities as a copyright holder, and the impact of open-access scholarly work, please describe one or two elements that you would consider when deciding if you will/will not share your work in the future."

Our overarching goal for library instruction on intellectual property rights is to better align the copyright culture of undergraduate research journals with informed scholarly communication practices. By giving students the power to decide how their work will be used by future scholars, they will see themselves as part of the scholarly process, which can also help in eliminating copyright-infringing behaviors in the future.

We are in the process of developing two additional workshops under the rubric of the Undergraduate Research Certificate: the first is on data management processes, including basic data-cleaning principles; and the second is on how students can manage their online scholarly presence by learning how to cite their publications properly for a resume/curriculum vitae, how to make their scholarly work findable in the institutional repository, and a basic introduction to scholarly profile systems such as Google Scholar and ORCiD.

CONCLUSION

There is recognition in academia that student publishing is growing exponentially across disciplines and is now being used as a pedagogical tool, both in academic disciplines and in the library. The 2013 ACRL white paper "Intersections of Scholarly Communication and Information Literacy: Creating Strategic Collaborations for a Changing Academic Environment" clearly reinforces the importance of information literacy instruction for those involved with undergraduate research journals, stating:

> Librarians who have become more involved with student-run journals find that working with undergraduate students as authors, editors, and publishers is an excellent way to teach about the economic, technological, and legal aspects of publishing, emphasizing the traditional life cycle of scholarly information.[40]

Teaching undergraduate students about intellectual property issues requires a balance between sharing and protecting scholarly work, otherwise we risk pushing them toward the side of protecting their own creative enterprises over sharing openly. Without instruction on how intellectual property directly affects their work and their concerns, students are left making decisions in a vacuum, or worse, not making any decisions at all. The ACRL Framework proclaims that students "have a greater role and responsibility in creating new knowledge, in understanding the contours and the changing dynamics of the world of information, and in using information, data, and scholarship ethically."[41] The experiential learning that is taking place in undergraduate research programs across all disciplines is fertile ground for teaching intellectual property rights at a level that directly impacts the undergraduate student. The librarians' parallel role at the intersections of scholarly communication and information literacy provokes us to create learning opportunities with the explicit intention of moving the neophyte researcher along a novice-to-expert continuum to "complete" the research process.

Ultimately, we are left with one question: Will students be surprised by the mechanisms in place in existing publishing culture, and will they work to change them?

NOTES

1. George D. Kuh, *High-Impact Educational Practices: What They Are, Who Has Access to Them, and Why They Matter* (Washington, DC: Association of American Colleges and Universities, 2008), 19.

2. Carleton College, "Starting Point: Teaching Entry Level Geoscience," https://serc.carleton.edu/introgeo/studentresearch/What.html.

3. Sean M. Stone and M. Sara Lowe, "Who Is Citing Undergraduate Theses in Institutional Digital Repositories? Implications for Scholarship and Information Literacy," *College & Undergraduate Libraries* 21, no. 3 (2014): 345–59, doi:10.1080/10691316.2014.929065.

4. Note: Student publications are increasingly experimenting with multimedia publications, but this chapter focuses on text as the medium.

5. *The Economist*, "How Does Copyright Work in Space?" May 29, 2013, https://www.economist.com/the-economist-explains/2013/05/22/how-does-copyright-work-in-space.

6. Case Western Reserve University, Kelvin Smith Library, "Common Copyright Myths," http://library.case.edu/copyright/cmyths.html.

7. Gene Quinn, "USC Launches Its First IP Course for Undergrads," IP Watchdog, 2017, www.ipwatchdog.com/2017/09/27/usc-launches-first-ip-course-undergrads/id=88341/.

8. David Kline et al., *The Intangible Advantage: Understanding Intellectual Property in the New Economy* (Los Angeles: Michelson 20MM Foundation, 2016).

9. Michelson 20MM Foundation, "Intellectual Property," November 7, 2016, https://www.youtube.com/playlist?list=PLDE5rhcpiAt_GDTYORzG11FAVhrHzkEjE.

10. The term "librarian" is meant to be taken broadly to include subject liaisons as well as functional specialists in copyright, scholarly communications, and information literacy and instruction.

11. Merinda Kaye Hensley and Heidi R. Johnson, "The Library as Collaborator in Student Publishing: An Index and Review of Undergraduate Research Journals," *Scholarship and Practice of Undergraduate Research* (In Press, 2018a). TBD ~24 typescript pages.

12. Merinda Kaye Hensley and Heidi R. Johnson, "Undergraduate Research Journal Data, 2014–2015," University of Illinois at Urbana-Champaign, 2018, https://doi.org/10.13012/B2IDB-5348256_V1.

13. Association of College and Research Libraries, "Framework for Information Literacy for Higher Education," 2016, www.ala.org/acrl/standards/ilframework.

14. Library Publishing Coalition, "Directory," 2018, https://librarypublishing.org/resources/.

15. Scalar, https://scalar.me/anvc/scalar/; and Omeka, https://omeka.org/.

16. Jody Condit Fagan and Malia Willey, "The Discoverability of Award-Winning Undergraduate Research in History: Implications for Academic Libraries," *College & Undergraduate Libraries* 25, no. 2 (2018): 164–86, doi:10.1080/1069 1316.2018.1456994.

17. Inclusion is contingent upon an advisory board of which at least two members have a PhD or equivalent: https://doaj.org/publishers.

18. Alexis D. Hart, *How to Start an Undergraduate Research Journal* (Washington, DC: Council on Undergraduate Research, 2012).

19. Kolb's experiential learning theory defines experiential learning as "the process whereby knowledge is created through the transformation of experience. Knowledge results from the combination of grasping and transforming experience." David Kolb, *Experiential Learning* (Englewood Cliffs, NJ: Prentice-Hall, 1984).

20. Association of College and Research Libraries, "Framework."

21. Sarah Hare and Cara Evanson, "Information Privilege Outreach for Undergraduate Students," *College & Research Libraries* 79, no. 6 (2018): 726–36.

22. Char Booth, "Open Access as Pedagogy," *info-mational* (blog), July 29, 2013, https://infomational.com/2013/07/29/open-access-as-pedagogy/.

23. For more on experiential learning, see Janet Eyler, "The Power of Experiential Education," *Liberal Education* 95, no. 4 (2009), https://www.aacu.org/publications-research/periodicals/power-experiential-education.

24. Jesse Stommel, "Who Controls Your Dissertation?" Chronicle Vitae, January 7, 2015, https://chroniclevitae.com/news/852-who-controls-your-dissertation.

25. University of Illinois at Urbana Champaign, Office of Undergraduate Research, https://undergradresearch.illinois.edu/; and University of Illinois at Urbana-Champaign, Undergraduate Research Certificate Program, https://undergradresearch.illinois.edu/students/research-certificate.html.

26. In an attempt to limit content to the most impactful decisions that undergraduate researchers need to make, we don't provide an in-depth overview of basic copyright or the underlying reasons for copyright. Instead, we choose to use our limited time of ninety minutes to model our fair use analysis to situations that apply directly to students' upcoming publication.

27. Cult of Pedagogy: "Anticipatory set (noun): a brief portion of a lesson given at the very beginning to get students' attention, activate prior knowledge,

and prepare them for the day's learning. Also known as advance organizer, hook, or set induction," https://www.cultofpedagogy.com/anticipatory-set/.

28. The language used here comes from Case Western Reserve University, "Common Copyright Myths," http://library.case.edu/copyright/cmyths.html.

29. Assessing prior knowledge inspired by Melissa Bowles-Terry and Cassandra Kvenild, *Classroom Assessment Techniques for Librarians* (Chicago: American Library Association, 2015), chap. 1.

30. Monica Kast and Taylor Potter, "After Three Years, Anthony Mazur Wins Ownership of His Photos, and His Former High School Has Promised to Stop Making Students Sign Over Their Copyright," Student Press Law Center, March 19, 2018, www.splc.org/article/2018/03/anthony-mazur-lawsuit.

31. Kevin P. Seeber, "The Failed Pedagogy of Punishment: Moving Discussions of Plagiarism beyond Detection and Discipline," in *Critical Library Pedagogy Handbook*, ed. N. Pagowsky and K. McElroy (Chicago: Association of College and Research Libraries, 2016), 131–38.

32. Association of Research Libraries, "Fair Use Fundamentals," http://fairuseweek.org/wp-content/uploads/2015/02/ARL-FUW-Infographic-r4.pdf.

33. The worksheet is based on the work of the University of Minnesota, "A Map of Use Issues," https://www.lib.umn.edu/copyright/usemap.

34. Chris Argyris, *Increasing Leadership Effectiveness* (New York: Wiley, 1976).

35. Creative Commons, https://creativecommons.org/.

36. *Re:Search: The Undergraduate Literary Criticism Journal at the University of Illinois*, https://ugresearchjournals.illinois.edu/index.php/ujlc/about/submissions#copyrightNotice.

37. Cult of Pedagogy, "Constructivism," https://www.cultofpedagogy.com/constructivism/.

38. SPARC, https://sparcopen.org/.

39. University of Illinois at Urbana-Champaign, Illinois Digital Environment for Access to Learning and Scholarship (IDEALS), "Undergraduate Research," https://www.ideals.illinois.edu/handle/2142/50121.

40. Association of College and Research Libraries, Working Group on Intersections of Scholarly Communication and Information Literacy, "Intersections of Scholarly Communication and Information Literacy: Creating Strategic Collaborations for a Changing Academic Environment," 2013, www.acrl.ala.org/intersections/.

41. Association of College and Research Libraries, "Intersections of Scholarly Communication."

ANALI PERRY

7

Building Copyright Confidence in Instructional Designers

COLLEGES AND UNIVERSITIES ARE INCREASINGLY DIRECTING their efforts towards online educational initiatives in order to expand their reach, improve educational opportunities and outcomes, and compete for potential students at scale. Staff and personnel with expertise in online learning platforms and new technologies, as well as a solid foundation in online learning pedagogies, are in high demand. The field of instructional design is rapidly growing to meet this need, producing instructional designers with these critically necessary skills. Instructional designers usually provide support to teaching faculty in developing and optimizing content for online instruction. They may also be responsible for providing quality control for online content. In this role, they often find themselves in the position of advising on or enforcing copyright compliance, despite rarely having had formal training in copyright and how it applies to educational situations. Since each instructional designer usually works with several faculty members, there is an opportunity to build capacity among this constituency and improve copyright compliance in a large number of courses. To do this, instructional designers need targeted copyright education that builds their confidence in evaluating common educational scenarios.

In this case study, I will describe my unique situation as an embedded librarian among the instructional designers in EdPlus at Arizona State University (ASU). First, I will provide an overview of the typical responsibilities and copyright needs of instructional designers, followed by a discussion of the methods I use for providing targeted copyright instruction, and finally I will conclude with ideas for potential next steps in providing this instruction.

As the scholarly communication librarian, I am the de facto copyright expert at ASU. There is otherwise little centralized copyright assistance for faculty and staff. In order to fill this need, I created a library guide that provides general information about copyright and fair use, specific resources targeted at instructors and authors, and links to reliable sources for further information.[1] Our Office of General Counsel recommends my library guide as a resource for copyright questions that are asked of them. I regularly teach copyright workshops—specifically copyright for instructors and copyright for authors—provide individual consultations, and answer most reference questions that deal with copyright issues. While I am not a lawyer, I usually have sufficient knowledge of copyright law to guide others through a copyright analysis to come to their own conclusions and, if not, refer them to resources that can help. Over the past few years, I have received an increasing number of copyright questions from instructional designers around the university, specifically from those affiliated with EdPlus.

EdPlus is a rapidly growing division of ASU. When the unit formed in 2011, it managed 22 programs serving 5,402 students. By 2017 there were 140 programs, with over 42,000 students.[2] Additionally, the work of EdPlus has expanded from managing traditional online degree programs such as ASU Online to exploring nontraditional learning pathways, such as the Global Freshman Academy and the Mastercard Foundation's Mastercard Scholars Program. EdPlus is located at Skysong, a public-private partnership with ASU, in Scottsdale, Arizona. While this location is home to some ASU departments, it also includes office space for innovative companies and startups, provides mentorship programs for students and businesses to work together, and rents out meeting space. However, classes are not offered there. I had led copyright and fair use workshops at Skysong a few times and had started to develop relationships with some of the employees of EdPlus there. The EdPlus leadership contacted me to discuss copyright considerations and request my assistance in finding open content just days before our launch of the Global Freshman Academy, a series of massively open online courses (MOOCs) in 2015. In 2016, the ASU Library assigned a librarian to work at Skysong as an on-site liaison to EdPlus, so as to provide a direct connection to library resources and services for this rapidly innovating team.

The ASU Library is in the midst of a major remodeling of the Hayden Library, our university's largest library building and the home of more than ninety personnel. This remodeling has required a relocation of the majority of our print collection to other libraries and high-density storage facilities, as well as finding temporary and permanent workspace for all but a few library staff who remain to provide services at Hayden during construction. Most personnel were relocated to other library locations, but EdPlus offered space for another librarian at Skysong. Since one of their greatest information needs was copyright and open licensing, I was the natural choice. My move to Skysong presented me with a great opportunity to explore embedded librarianship. Embedded librarians are often located in close physical proximity to a specific group, allowing them to become trusted members of the community.[3] My goals were to develop a closer relationship with the instructional designers at EdPlus and explore methods, both formal and informal, for improving their understanding of copyright. I packed up my office, which had been in the largest library at ASU's largest campus, serving 50,000 students during the semester, and moved to Skysong. The environment there is very different from a traditional academic library setting, with more of a corporate tone. Employees work in an open-office arrangement in cubicles or workstations, but there is plenty of natural lighting (a pleasant change from my prior basement office), rooms for small and large-group meetings and events, a staff lounge, a workout room, and regularly scheduled professional development programs.

EdPlus has welcomed us with open arms. We are invited to attend monthly group meetings and were added to EdPlus's Slack instance, which allows us to see updates, news, and the general conversations that take place among the staff, including what issues concern them and what challenges they face. This helps us to assess their information needs. I had only a surface understanding of the roles that instructional designers fill before moving to EdPlus, but working among them for the past year has deepened my knowledge.

WHAT DOES AN INSTRUCTIONAL DESIGNER DO?

The realm of online education has evolved rapidly, and it is clear that many of the techniques for teaching in a face-to-face classroom do not translate well to an online environment. There is a need to explore different pedagogical approaches and new ways to present learning materials in order to keep students engaged and to improve educational outcomes. The Bill and Melinda Gates Foundation Report, "Instructional Design in Higher Education," breaks the general responsibilities of instructional designers into four roles.[4] First, they are designers, which involves creating new courses or redeveloping old courses, creating curriculum and professional development for instructors, and providing quality control and accessibility compliance. Second, they are managers, providing project management for developing courses, promoting instructional design services, and serving as liaisons to administrators, instructors, curriculum designers, and information technology. Third, they are trainers, teaching faculty about new technology tools and online pedagogy techniques, and providing professional development on course design, curriculum, assessment, active learning, and theory and practice. Finally, they provide support, resolving technical problems and instructional challenges, and migrating face-to-face courses to an online system. In sum, instructional designers apply their understanding of learning, teaching, and technology to online course development in order to make it more meaningful to the students.[5] The titles of instructional designers vary, and the position may be called e-learning developer, educational technologist, or instructional technologist.

Most instructional designers have a blend of teaching and technology backgrounds, and the majority have at least a master's degree (see figure 7.1). Indeed, advanced degrees in instructional design or technology are becoming more common.[6] The instructional designers and staff at ASU come from teaching, library, or technology backgrounds.[7] They work closely with faculty and instructors to develop online learning modules that follow current educational best practices. They coach faculty and instructors on best practices for online engagement and learning, improving student outcomes, and leveraging technology to improve the teaching and learning experience. While the instructor leads and develops the syllabus and general content of the course, the instructional designer coaches the instructor on issues such as articulating learning objectives, developing appropriate assessment instruments, and recommending the best tools for the best outcomes. The designer also works with the instructor to determine and develop the best supplemental material to use, including video lectures, tutorials, and any other learning objects that are best suited to the material. Therefore, instructional designers are in a unique position to help promote good copyright practice and encourage their faculty partners to do the same.

In my experience, instructional designers' understanding of copyright is spotty at best and is based on community practices, urban legends, outdated classroom guidelines, and departmental policies; this imperfect understanding is consistent with that of university faculty and instructors in general.[8]

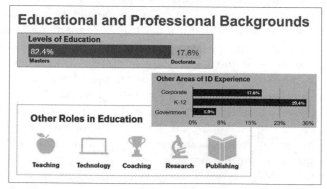

FIGURE 7.1
Instructional Designers' Educational Background

Instructional designers struggle to find time for professional development while balancing a heavy workload with a constant emphasis on speed of delivery. Since ASU does not include information about copyright in its training for instructors and the Office of General Counsel does not assist with copyright inquiries, the most reliable resource for copyright and fair use questions from faculty, staff, and students is the ASU Library.

SPECIFIC COPYRIGHT NEEDS

Higher education is grappling with the application of common copyright practice to a rapidly changing online learning environment where even our definitions of "student" and "classroom" are evolving. These definitions matter when determining which exceptions to the exclusive rights of copyright holders apply to any given situation. Section 110 of the U.S. Copyright Act, known as the classroom use provision, makes it possible for teachers at non-profit institutions to perform or display copyrighted works, such as showing a film or displaying a work of art. The Technology, Education and Copyright Harmonization (TEACH) Act of 2002 attempted to cope with the transition to online learning, but its lengthy list of institutional and technological requirements makes it impractical for most situations. The licenses for online library resources typically restrict use to "authorized users," which is usually defined as currently enrolled students, faculty, and staff. Access is granted through physical presence on a campus or through IP authentication using an institutionally provided user name and password. Increasingly, institutions must rely on the doctrine of fair use, section 107, in order to incorporate and adapt copyrighted materials in online learning environments. While fair use is a powerful and flexible doctrine, it is widely misunderstood and is unfortunately perceived as an unreliable tool.

EdPlus has a specific and complex set of needs with regard to understanding and complying with copyright. Its learning situations are nearly exclusive to online education and are only rarely face-to-face. While the ASU Online programs target officially enrolled students following a traditional degree path, many of the other initiatives do not. Professional development and accreditation courses targeting business partners are offered for a fee, so there is some question whether they are for-profit offerings. There are also an ever-increasing number of programs designed to expand educational opportunities to learners around the world who are not officially enrolled students. The Global Freshman Academy (GFA), for example, is a set of first-year courses offered on the edX platform as MOOCs, which means that anyone, anywhere, can register for these courses. If students register for one of these courses using the verified identity option, which has a small fee, they can choose to pay an additional fee to receive official ASU credit at any time, including after successfully completing and passing the course. Receiving a passing grade (a C or higher) in eight courses qualifies as a full freshman year and guarantees admission to ASU. The credits are recorded as full ASU credit on a student's transcript, so the student can transfer those credits to another university if he or she desires.[9]

Another example is ASU's participation in the Mastercard Foundation Scholars program, a ten-year initiative to educate and prepare young people (primarily from sub-Saharan Africa) to lead change and make a positive social impact in their communities.[10] EdPlus received a grant from the Mastercard Foundation to design the Baobab Scholars Community Platform, a custom learning and social networking platform that delivers a personalized learning experience based on each Baobab Scholar's interests.[11] Baobab was fully implemented in fall 2016 and includes learning modules, discussion boards, and other electronic resources designed to help each Scholar further their personal and academic development. A key component of this program is a commitment to lifelong learning and building a sustained community, so this network will continue to be available to Scholars after they complete their education, including access to curated resources and educational content.

These examples illustrate some of the complex copyright issues that arise: a mixture of nonprofit and for-profit activities; the use of closed learning management systems as well as MOOCs on an open platform; officially enrolled students with access to library databases versus learners around the world with dubious library access; and hosting and delivering content to students in other countries. Different copyright exceptions and provisions apply to each of these scenarios, and the instructional designers are in a position to build capacity for copyright best practices at scale.

LEARNING OBJECTIVES

My first steps to build confidence and capacity in my new community included discussing copyright documentation with the EdPlus compliance team and assisting with a copyright audit of a course. Then I determined that the immediate coaching needs were a basic overview of copyright, establishing that copyright and attribution are separate issues, developing a deeper understanding of fair use and an increased comfort level for a fair use evaluation, clarifying the situations where the TEACH Act may apply, and increasing the understanding of Creative Commons (CC) licenses and strategies for searching for openly licensed content. These priorities were also informed by the common general questions I've received regarding copyright, including clarifying what is protected by copyright and what is in the public domain online, interpreting website terms of use and digital rights management/Digital Millennium Copyright Act issues, and explaining attribution best practices.

As expected, I receive the most questions about fair use. The easiest questions to answer deal with whether it is acceptable to link to an outside, freely available source or to use platform-provided embed codes, such as embedding a YouTube video. However, most fair use questions require walking through an analysis of the four factors of fair use, and it became clear that the instructional designers were unsure about their ability to do this. They also feel pressure from instructors, usually faculty, who may take a more cavalier approach to fair use than is advisable. I do not typically receive any questions about the TEACH Act from instructional designers, but I have been able to identify situations where it is the most applicable copyright exception, despite its many detailed stipulations.

While many of the instructional designers are aware of Creative Commons licenses and know to specifically seek out CC-licensed content, they are not fully informed of the different license options and often need help interpreting their terms. For example, TED Talks are popular resources for online education, and are usually licensed with a CC-BY-NC-ND license.[12] Even so, instructional designers are unsure whether it's acceptable to download the video file of a TED Talk and upload it into a course management platform; whether they can use a TED Talk if a fee is charged for a course; and whether they can make a translation of the TED Talk's transcript.

I planned a variety of coaching opportunities using both formal and informal approaches to address these needs and improve core competencies among the instructional designers. My more formal approaches include planning traditional workshops and webinars on copyright, fair use, Creative Commons, and searching for openly licensed resources; creating targeted tutorials; and participating in team meetings. Informally, I have taken advantage of being embedded among the team and have made myself visible and available for informal conversations and for answering questions, in person, on e-mail, and on Slack.

HOW TO HELP

Informal Approaches

I had already been providing some copyright consultation and reference services to EdPlus prior to moving to Skysong, mainly via e-mail or referral. However, my physical proximity and increased visibility there have proven immensely valuable. My cubicle is situated among the instructional designers, which reduces the barriers to addressing informal questions and discussing instructional opportunities through casual conversation.

While I still receive some questions via e-mail, the majority of the online conversation with the team is done via Slack. Slack is a combination discussion board and instant messaging service; it provides a place for asynchronous conversation among groups of various sizes through subject- or team-focused channels, as well as the ability to direct message individuals or small groups. EdPlus added our library contingent to its Slack instance, and we were invited to the general channel (for everyone on the instance), the ASU-wide instructional design channel, and the EdPlus-only instructional design team, as well as the channels for open education initiatives. This access provides us with the opportunity to share relevant information to a wide group without cluttering our e-mail or needing an e-mail list. I can post relevant copyright news or resources to a targeted group, and often provide links to open repositories of content.

Slack is the method by which I answer the majority of copyright questions from EdPlus, using the direct message feature. Instructional designers now know that I am generally available on Slack, and they will send me questions. The instant message function is much easier than e-mail to tease out specific details in a back-and-forth conversation, and it allows me to easily link to references and to answer questions responsively.

FORMAL APPROACHES

The instructional designers at EdPlus have regularly scheduled monthly meetings in order to share information, provide updates on different projects, and celebrate accomplishments. There is a standard agenda template, and the library is fortunate to have a standing agenda slot each month for providing updates and information. I make a point to attend this meeting when I am available, and I include at least one targeted copyright resource for the participants—such as marketing an upcoming workshop or a Fair Use Week event, providing a link to a library guide, or mentioning a useful tool. The agenda is shared using Google Docs, so I can see in advance what topics are being discussed and I can target my updates to issues of immediate concern. For example, if I see that the Global Freshman Academy team is working on adding a new MOOC course, I might mention the OER (Open Educational Resource) Metafinder tool for locating open educational resources. I find that my physical presence at this meeting each month emphasizes my availability as a resource as well.

While the greatest concentration of instructional designers resides within EdPlus, instructional designers are also spread among the various colleges and schools at ASU. EdPlus hosts a quarterly meeting of all the instructional designers at the university. This meeting has a team-building emphasis, and again, my colleague and I are invited to participate. It has been a great opportunity to build relationships and make library services more visible, as well as position ourselves as reliable resources for information related to copyright.

EdPlus provides a regular schedule of the professional development opportunities that are available to ASU instructors and instructional designers, such as accessibility compliance and academic integrity using Eventbrite. By partnering with some of the EdPlus staff, I am able to plan workshops and list them on the existing schedule, as well as track registrations. I work with my library colleague as well as an EdPlus media manager with TEACH Act knowledge to present an in-person workshop that covers the basics of copyright, the TEACH Act, and fair use (see the "Copyright and Fair Use Workshop Outline"). We provided participants with a customized copyright analysis infographic and a standard fair use checklist (see figure 7.2). The workshop included group discussions of common scenarios encountered in online learning environments. We adapted this presentation to a webinar, which allowed us to incorporate polls to help us evaluate the attendees' previous knowledge and keep them engaged in the absence of a group discussion.

Copyright and Fair Use Workshop Outline

A. Learning objectives

1. Understand what copyright covers

2. Understand the relationship between copyright and attribution

B. What is copyright and what does it cover?

1. What types of works are covered by copyright?

2. Bundle of rights

- Copy

- Distribute

- Modify

- Perform/display

- Make derivative works

3. What is not covered by copyright?

4. What copyright exceptions do we use for education?

- Classroom use (section 110a)

- TLACH Act (section 110b)

- Fair use (section 107)

- Four factors:

  ◊ Purpose   ◊ Amount

  ◊ Nature   ◊ Effect

- Sample scenario—work through as a group

  ◊ An instructor is creating a Global Freshman Academy course on architecture and wants to include a photo of a Frank Lloyd Wright (d. 1959) building that he found on a blog. The blogger has not identified who took the picture or where it came from. Attempts to contact the blogger have resulted in no response.

- Breakout groups—use Scenarios handout, Checklist handout

- Report out/discussion

C. Resources/questions

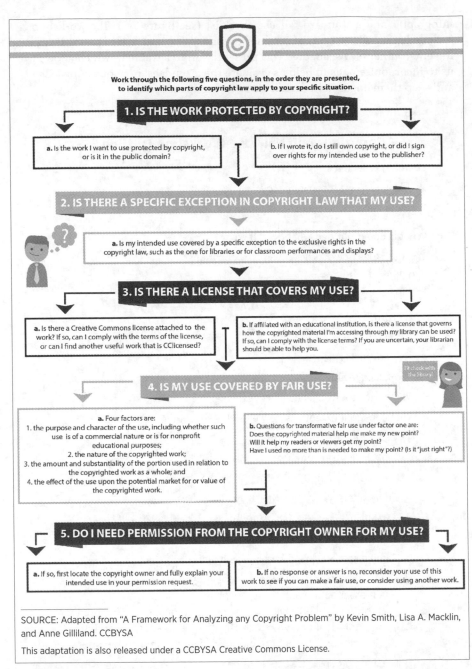

Work through the following five questions, in the order they are presented, to identify which parts of copyright law apply to your specific situation.

1. IS THE WORK PROTECTED BY COPYRIGHT?

a. Is the work I want to use protected by copyright, or is it in the public domain?

b. If I wrote it, do I still own copyright, or did I sign over rights for my intended use to the publisher?

2. IS THERE A SPECIFIC EXCEPTION IN COPYRIGHT LAW THAT MY USE?

a. Is my intended use covered by a specific exception to the exclusive rights in the copyright law, such as the one for libraries or for classroom performances and displays?

3. IS THERE A LICENSE THAT COVERS MY USE?

a. Is there a Creative Commons license attached to the work? If so, can I comply with the terms of the license, or can I find another useful work that is CC licensed?

b. If affiliated with an educational institution, is there a license that governs how the copyrighted material I'm accessing through my library can be used? If so, can I comply with the license terms? If you are uncertain, your librarian should be able to help you.

I'll check with the library!

4. IS MY USE COVERED BY FAIR USE?

a. Four factors are:
1. the purpose and character of the use, including whether such use is of a commercial nature or is for nonprofit educational purposes;
2. the nature of the copyrighted work;
3. the amount and substantiality of the portion used in relation to the copyrighted work as a whole; and
4. the effect of the use upon the potential market for or value of the copyrighted work.

b. Questions for transformative fair use under factor one are:
Does the copyrighted material help me make my new point?
Will it help my readers or viewers get my point?
Have I used no more than is needed to make my point? (Is it "just right"?)

5. DO I NEED PERMISSION FROM THE COPYRIGHT OWNER FOR MY USE?

a. If so, first locate the copyright owner and fully explain your intended use in your permission request.

b. If no response or answer is no, reconsider your use of this work to see if you can make a fair use, or consider using another work.

SOURCE: Adapted from "A Framework for Analyzing any Copyright Problem" by Kevin Smith, Lisa A. Macklin, and Anne Gilliland. CCBYSA

This adaptation is also released under a CCBYSA Creative Commons License.

FIGURE 7.2
Copyright Analysis Infographic

Creative Commons Licenses and Open Search Strategies Webinar Outline

A. Learning objectives

   1. Recognize when materials are under a Creative Commons license

   2. Describe the differences between CC licenses

   3. Accurately apply knowledge of CC licenses to the selection and use of materials

   4. Use effective search practices for finding openly licensed materials

B. Reasons for Creative Commons

C. Introduction to Creative Commons licenses, with a quick summary of each license

D. Knowledge check—poll

   1. If you wanted to make a change to a CC-licensed work, which license allows that?

      - CC-BY-SA

      - CC-BY-ND

      - CC-BY-ND-NC

E. Finding content

   1. Known content (e.g., specific articles or books)

   2. Unknown content (e.g., looking for images for a presentation)

F. Open Attribution Builder

   Knowledge check—poll

   1. You need a great image of a Tasmanian devil for a presentation. Which resource would you use to find a CC-licensed image?

      - OER MetaFinder

      - CC Search

      - Open Access Button

   2. You know about a perfect article to support an assignment in your course. Which of the following resources would you search in order to locate an openly available version of the article?

      - UnPaywall

      - HathiTrust

      - Internet Archive

We then presented a webinar providing an overview of Creative Commons licenses and recommending strategies for finding open content. We described each of the different CC licenses, and talked about different resources for different content types (such as text or images). Then we described advanced search strategies that enable limiting searches by license type in order to specifically find content that has fewer copyright restrictions. The outline of our presentation is included as "Creative Commons Licenses and Open Search Strategies Webinar Outline."

As part of its professional development training to improve faculty members' proficiency in online teaching and learning, EdPlus provides an ASU Online Faculty Center, which includes a series of self-paced learning modules called "10 Minutes to Excellence." Each module has a list of learning objectives that instructors should be able to achieve in under ten minutes. EdPlus invited me to contribute a copyright module, so I developed "Fair Use & Copyright for Online Instructors." The learning objectives for the module are:

- Explain a basic overview of fair use
- Identify the four factors of fair use
- Evaluate the likelihood that a use would be considered fair with regard to teaching
- Find where to get help regarding fair use

Finally, I created two library tutorials—one on using videos in teaching, and one specifically on fair use. While these were not specifically targeted to instructional designers, they address questions that the designers often receive, allowing them to pass these resources along to instructors who struggle with these concepts.

INDICATORS OF SUCCESS

One of the primary indicators of success is the increased level of engagement I have with the instructional designers at ASU. They are now much more familiar with the copyright resources that are available to them, and they are more likely to reach out to me with questions or to confirm their own evaluations. They frequently copy me on their responses to questions from faculty about copyright.

The evaluations and comments from our webinars and workshops have been positive. Most attendees report feeling more confident about achieving our learning objectives, and think that the webinar or workshop is a good use of their time. Their suggestions include adding more examples for discussion and more workshops on similar topics.

While I have not conducted a formal evaluation of my efforts here, anecdotally I can tell that it has made a difference. Several of the instructional designers have stated how helpful it is to have me available as a resource, and they report that their confidence in making copyright evaluations and problem-solving with copyright has grown significantly as a result of regularly working with me to address their specific situations. I am starting to see more complex questions from many of them now that they handle more of the basics on their own, and they are more likely to check in with me on the result of their evaluation rather than ask for help.

LESSONS LEARNED AND FUTURE IDEAS

Being embedded with the instructional designers has not been a one-way conversation. Prior to working at Skysong, I had only vague ideas of what instructional designers did. I have learned a great deal about their workflow and information needs through my relationships and conversations, and have gained a huge amount of respect for their field. I believe that I can improve my service by changing the types of information I provide and the ways I share it to better suit their needs.

One lesson is that in-person workshops do not provide a good return on the time investment for the number of people reached. There are rarely more than a dozen people who can attend. While I intend to continue offering workshops in person, I will limit these to once or twice a year, and instead offer webinars more often, especially now that I am more familiar with the technology and techniques. Additionally, I intend to record webinars and make them available for people to attend at their convenience.

Another important lesson is how best to provide reference information in ways that will be more practically useful. I have learned that the instructional designers are less likely to search the library web page or browse a library guide, and are much more likely to use their internal reference library, using a tool called Guru, which is where they keep and share information with their team. I have been given access to their team's library and can now add content in ways that will fit within their own workflows and project management cycles.

In the future, there is a need for a better method for documenting copyright decisions, such as fair use justifications, permissions granted, and licenses used. I plan to help develop a workflow for documenting these decisions in a standardized way for new projects. I'd also like to incorporate a copyright module into the regular training opportunities provided by EdPlus, such as the Masterclass for Teaching Online.[13] This two-week workshop for online instructors is offered on a quarterly basis and discusses best practices for online learning.

CONCLUSION

Embedded librarianship has been a growing trend in the profession for several years, but as a scholarly communication librarian, I had not expected to be embedded anywhere. My move to Skysong to work alongside instructional designers has been a valuable experience. Learning more about the work of instructional designers has given me insight into how I can help improve their understanding of copyright and fair use principles in a more meaningful way than I would have otherwise. I believe that developing a strong working relationship built on mutual understanding and respect has enabled me to be proactive in addressing their information needs. Informal conversations with guidance and coaching through the particular copyright situations faced by instructional designers have greatly improved their confidence in making their own evaluations and dealing with faculty. As libraries look toward the information needs of their community, I recommend that they specifically target the instructional designers at their institutions.

NOTES

1. Arizona State University, "Copyright Library Guide," libguides.asu.edu/copyright.
2. EdPlus, "Who We Are," edplus.asu.edu/who-we-are.
3. Kathy Drewes and Nadine Hoffman, "Academic Embedded Librarianship: An Introduction," *Public Services Quarterly* 6, no. 2–3 (September 14, 2010): 75–82, https://doi.org/10.1080/15228959.2010.498773.
4. Intentional Futures, "Instructional Design in Higher Education: A Report on the Role, Workflow, and Experience of Instructional Designers," April 2016, intentionalfutures.com/wp-content/uploads/2017/08/Instructional-Design-in-Higher-Education-Report.pdf.
5. Sean Michael Morris, "Instructional Designers Are Teachers," Hybrid Pedagogy, April 12, 2018, hybridpedagogy.org/instructional-designers-are-teachers/.
6. Sharon O'Malley, "Still a Mystery," Inside Higher Ed, August 2, 2017, www.insidehighered.com/digital-learning/article/2017/08/02/what-do-instructional-designers-do.
7. "What Do Instructional Designers Do?" ASU EdPlus Lunch and Learn Presentation, August 2, 2017.
8. Nancy Sims, "Lies, Damned Lies, and Copyright (Mis)Information: Empowering Faculty by Addressing Key Points of Confusion," Association of College and Research Libraries Conference Proceedings, 2011, p. 15, www.ala.org/acrl/sites/ala.org.acrl/files/content/conferences/confsandpreconfs/national/2011/papers/lies_damned_lies.pdf.

9. Arizona State University, "Global Freshman Academy," gfa.asu.edu/.
10. Arizona State University, Office of University Initiatives, "Mastercard Foundation Scholars Program," ui.asu.edu/projects/mastercard-scholars.
11. Arizona State University, Office of University Initiatives, "Baobab Scholars Community Platform," ui.asu.edu/projects/scholars-community-platform.
12. TED, "TED Talks Usage Policy," www.ted.com/about/our-organization/our-policies-terms/ted-talks-usage-policy.
13. Eventbrite, "Master Class for Teaching Online," https://www.eventbrite.com/e/master-class-for-teaching-online-july-2018-tickets-39562843530.

STEPHANIE DAVIS-KAHL
and KAREN SCHMIDT

8

Copyright Services at a Liberal Arts College

A Liberal Arts College Perspective

THE COPYRIGHT LANDSCAPE AT A SMALLER LIBERAL ARTS UNI-versity can look substantially different from that at larger research institutions, both in scope and in how it is supported. Larger universities will have multiple copyright and permissions issues, due to the sheer size of the faculty and research staff and the abundance of grants. In addition, there are very likely to be campus-based attorneys whose responsibility it is to mediate these issues. In contrast, smaller liberal arts institutions generally have fewer numbers of copyright and permissions issues and are less likely to have on-site legal staff. But the faculty at smaller institutions most often earn their PhD or other terminal degrees from large research institutions, and may bring along with them the expectation that attorneys with formal copyright and permissions training will be readily available. The realities of more constrained legal support can sometimes create challenges to addressing important questions of policy and protocol.

In this chapter, the authors consider the copyright and permissions environment of Illinois Wesleyan University (IWU), a small liberal arts university located in Bloomington, Illinois. With some 1,800 students and 160 full-time faculty, IWU is not unique among many liberal arts institutions in its experiences with and approaches to addressing copyright and rights and permissions for its students, faculty, and staff. We offer an overview of the opportunities and challenges of working with copyright in this environment, along with specific examples that reflect these realities.

THE LEGAL LANDSCAPE

IWU has an established contract with the local corporation counsel, who serve as advisers for a broad array of legal issues that the university may encounter, from student life to athletics to property acquisition. Copyright and rights and permissions are occasionally referred to this legal team, and there is one attorney who takes the lead on intellectual property questions. Permission to connect to this legal counsel is handled through the Provost's Office to track activities. It has been helpful for the university copyright officer (UCO) to work with campus legal counsel to establish some mutually agreed-upon operating principles that help the UCO gauge the level of risk in managing copyright and permission questions without constantly seeking legal counsel.

With this as the foundation, the largest portion of copyright work at IWU is handled by the UCO, who is also the university librarian. Linking copyright to the portfolio of the university librarian is a tradition that extends back to 1994. At that time, acting on the advice of the university counsel, the provost established policies and procedures for copyright compliance. These policies initially addressed the copyright concerns regarding coursepacks, with the university librarian named as the primary consultant, especially with regard to copying materials for course reserves. This work has evolved along with the emergence of digital content and open access. Hosting this work within the library creates beneficial connections between the library and teaching faculty in classroom and research activities. While coursepacks have dwindled rapidly over the past few years, some faculty continue to use them. The copyright conversations surrounding coursepack content create opportunities to educate the faculty about the library's digital and print collection resources, and alert the library faculty to possible gaps in the collections. The faculty's research activities bring colleagues to both our university librarian and our scholarly communications librarian for advice on topics such as publisher agreements, posting published research on the IWU institutional repository, and requests for assistance in securing permission for image use in scholarly articles. Each of these interactions is an opportunity to discuss open access initiatives and the importance of publisher policies. In 2015, the provost invited the university librarian and the scholarly communications librarian to help develop an intellectual property policy that would cover copyright, recommended licenses, patents, and inventions. This policy was added to the IWU faculty handbook in 2015[1] and has served as the basis of conversations with our entrepreneurship program and the Small Business Development Center.

A challenge in this scenario is the need for some foundational copyright training for the university copyright officer, along with continuing education. At IWU, the provost has provided funding for the university librarian to attend a national copyright conference. This meeting provides training from well-established library leaders whose professional work speaks directly to academic copyright and intellectual policy issues. E-mail lists, blogs, and robust websites from large universities sustain the education beyond the conference.[2] The IWU library has been fortunate to be able to bring copyright experts to campus every two or three years to speak to our students and faculty about specific issues (e.g., music copyright, which is of immediate interest to our School of Music and School of Theatre Arts), and these connections with experts have also facilitated occasional discussions about thorny problems that arise. On the IWU campus, faculty copyright interactions fall into a variety of different categories. A sampling of these are discussed in the sections below and are followed by case studies.

PERMISSION TO USE IMAGES

In common with the faculty at larger institutions, liberal arts faculty are active researchers whose scholarly output spans the usual range of presentations, journal articles, chapters, and books. The use of illustrative material in conference presentations and publishing brings with it the opportunity to educate the faculty about the options that are available through the public domain and Creative Commons.[3] Equally, it provides a platform for discussing the concept of fair use and assisting faculty in understanding and applying the nuances of the four-factor fair use test.[4] The library faculty at IWU push toward the most liberal interpretation of fair use, and keeping the balance tipped in favor of the public interest. However, publishers and journal editors will not always view this in the same way. Their own legal counsel will be looking at image use through the lens of risk assessment, and read the four factor test in a different manner. As a result, publishers often will require permission to use their images and place the responsibility of obtaining this permission on the faculty author, who then turns to the UCO for assistance.

Researching and adequately documenting the rights and permissions process poses certain challenges. The publisher with whom the faculty member is contracting may not provide enough information to make an informed inquiry (e.g., mode of distribution, print run, or transfer rights.) In addition, the inquiries to copyright holders for permission to use the content in an article are sometimes not answered, and the faculty member needs to consider alternatives. At times, the cost of using the image is prohibitive. Paying for the cost of the use of the image from campus funds may need to be negotiated if there is not a specified pool of money for faculty development and publishing support. At IWU, publication fees originally were provided by sharing expenses between the university library and the Office of the Provost. As these kinds of publishing costs became more common, the campus faculty development office created a publication expense pool to assist with the payment of copyright clearance and reproduction costs, submission and open access fees, and the costs associated with copyediting, indexing, and illustrations. The faculty make application to the faculty development committee as needed, and the UCO and the scholarly communications librarian assist in negotiations as needed.

One of the more complex situations at IWU arose with a classics professor whose journal article included eighteen images of a famous contemporary person. The journal publisher required detailed documentation of the author's having obtained usage rights or asserting public domain rights. Each one of these images added significantly to the written content, and each was a separate and sometimes highly involved negotiation. For example, the use of one of the images required that the archives holding the copyright had to have final approval of the publication copy before it was published. For the use of another image, there was no response despite repeated inquiries; consequently, our professor enlisted the aid of an artist who created a rendition of the image that reflected—but did not copy—the details that were being discussed in the research article. Organizing the details and the required documentation for this article to be published took many hours, resulting in a successful publication and a rich education for the university librarian on rights and permissions.

UNAUTHORIZED USE OF SCHOLARLY CONTENT BY ANOTHER SCHOLAR/AUTHOR

A surprising number of concerns are registered by faculty scholars who believe their research has been appropriated by another researcher and used in a publication without their authorization. These situations pose a number of investigatory challenges. Understanding the formal research relationship, if any, and reviewing the partnership agreements are fundamental. The research offices on other campuses can assist in understanding ethics and agreements, and contact with the publishers is critical. Occasionally, it is necessary to involve the campus legal counsel to send cease and desist warnings.

An untenured faculty member in the sciences came to the university librarian with significant concerns that his photographs of a rare species had been placed into a repository, and one of the images had been published without his knowledge, permission, or attribution. This occurred at a university in another country, and the actions had been overseen by a senior researcher with whom the IWU faculty member had studied and worked. Because of the international aspects and the possible impact on the IWU faculty member's scholarly record, we engaged our campus attorney to ask that the images be removed from the online archive and that appropriate attribution be inserted in the publication. While stressful, the situation was successfully resolved after several months.

POSSIBLE PLAGIARISM IN STUDENT WORK

From time to time, a faculty member will ask for assistance in determining if a student has used copyrighted material without attribution. The IWU campus does not subscribe to TurnItIn or similar plagiarism software, but the ability to search full-text online content often serves the same purpose. These inquiries provide the opportunity for targeted information literacy instruction with a class or a student.

An example of the work we are able to do as library faculty can be seen in a request from a professor who received a student research paper assignment that included many instances of phrasing that were unlike any previous writings from this student. Using online resources and advanced search options, library faculty were able to identify a number of articles that were used without attribution. The student's case was handled as an academic integrity issue, and we were given the opportunity to work with the student on the use of citations in scholarly work.

Issues with student plagiarism are distinct from students inadvertently engaging in copyright infringement. Students receive guidance throughout their IWU academic careers about the importance of academic honesty. Nevertheless, in the "sharing economy" that is now the norm for many young adults, images and other content that are easily discoverable on the Web do not at first glance appear to have any of the more scholarly restrictions associated with appropriating content from scholarly journals and books. A case in point was a student newspaper article about a mumps outbreak, with an accompanying photograph that showed swollen salivary glands. The student editors were surprised to receive a formal takedown notice and an invoice for $1,500 for publishing a photo that turned out to be part of a large commercial gallery of photographs. The faculty advisor successfully argued for a lower usage cost, and the UCO was able to use this example productively in discussing online image search tools, public domain, and the general meaning of copyright and why it matters. As is noted later in this chapter, these lessons also come into play in publishing students' research in student journals.

USE OF AUDIO AND VIDEO

A number of situations can arise with audio and video content. Faculty may ask to post personal recordings of commercial content to online course pages. Films that do not have appropriate public performance rights may be shown and advertised to the public at large as part of a community event. And faculty may inadvertently use video or audio without permission in presentations that end up on the open web. Likewise, faculty who supervise music and theater students frequently contend with students' family members taping and uploading concert material on YouTube, tagged with the names of the university, the professor, and the student. Music copyright is complex, and copyright officers need to be aware of how BMI, ASCAP, and SESAC licenses are maintained and used, and become familiar with synchronization rights. Guest lecturers can also pose challenges if the university decides to post their presentations without prior agreements.

In a recent situation, the music school asked that a policy be developed that they could share with audience members who came to listen to student recitals. The policy was necessary because of problems of posting on YouTube from a handful of individuals who had disregarded written notices not to record recitals on cell phones. Working through the policy provided the opportunity for a number of faculty and staff to come together to craft an overarching document that articulates campus policies and procedures. Given the broad scope of the document, it was reviewed and approved by the campus legal counsel.

In another interesting case, a student work group put together a video that addressed students sharing private information online, with possible negative consequences. The video used a popular rock song without permission. This video was submitted to Educause for a student video award. With the potential of the video being shared online, the university librarian agreed to seek permission for the use of the song. Eschewing ASCAP and BMI and other music publishing options, the artist whose song was used had chosen to retain all rights to his work, and he personally endorsed the use of his song in the video. For both the students and the university librarian, this was a rare and instructive look at how the music industry works and the complexities that surround music publishing.

EDUCATION AND AWARENESS ABOUT PUBLISHING CONTRACTS AND AUTHOR RIGHTS

Reviewing contracts prior to publishing, as well as after publishing to host on IWU's institutional repository, are two services that have grown steadily over the past decade. There are numerous examples of our work with faculty on reviewing contracts and publisher policies; this section is a compilation of our observations on the teachable moments and challenges in this area.

As outreach for faculty participation in the institutional repository increases, and as open access to scholarly literature becomes more accepted across more disciplines, the faculty at IWU seem to understand that there are choices under their control when it comes to publication rights and venues. While there are, and will continue to be, disciplinary differences between the sciences, social sciences, and humanities with regard to open access, open data, and participation in services such as the institutional repository, Research-Gate, and Academia.edu, generational differences are less apparent. Faculty members' awareness and understanding of the scholarly publishing landscape is often narrow and specific to their discipline, and sometimes to their experiences with publishing with mentors or advisors in graduate school.

Similarly, faculty often hold onto the misconception that copyright is a monolith without flexibility, instead of understanding copyright as a continuum of choices across five domains (also known as the "bundle of rights").[5] This all-or-nothing approach also extends to concepts like open access and Creative Commons, both of which introduce authorial control of choices and greater visibility for a finished product. Faculty members may not be accustomed to the degree of critical thinking required by the array of choices and decisions when considering long-term access to their work. Encouraging faculty to think about not only the long-term trajectory of their research agenda, but also the trajectory of how they *share* their work is a long-term process that often necessitate a series of conversations to raise their awareness and capitalize on teachable moments. Another challenge is that faculty often conflate copyright guidelines for the use of materials in the classroom with copyright guidelines and publisher policies for their own research, not understanding that while the two are interrelated, there are different considerations. Oftentimes, faculty are frustrated at having to ask for permission to use copyrighted materials in a coursepack or electronic reserves; at the same time, they value the royalties that result from faculty at other institutions using their research in similar course-based ways. The financial aspects of scholarly publishing and the use of scholarly materials are often outside a faculty member's purview; this is why educating library advisory committees, faculty, and administrators about the costs of publishing and using scholarship is important.

Every year we have additional faculty members from across the university who express interest in establishing their own site within our institutional repository; this can be attributed to a number of factors. We create and maintain these sites for faculty, updating them usually once a year or as needed. We are responsive to faculty requests for changes, and over time this has built up a certain amount of goodwill. Another factor is the increasing need for faculty to have an online presence that communicates their research agenda, publication history, and their work with students. The sites' audiences include grant funders, prospective students, faculty and administrators at other institutions, and the general public.

STUDENTS

As undergraduate research efforts grow on liberal arts campuses, so do opportunities for students to share their work outside the boundaries of the campus. Undergraduate research, when a student engages in deep research over an extended period of time advised by a faculty mentor, is a highly valued activity across nearly all disciplines, and is becoming a major selling point to prospective students who are looking for opportunities to distinguish themselves for future employers and graduate school admission. Students produce a multitude of products to share, and have choices about how and where to disseminate their work. Increasingly, students also bring with them experiences as creators in non-academic contexts, that is, as YouTubers, podcasters, writers, performers, and so on. Furthermore, students with experience sharing their work prior to college are also more attuned to the notion of open content, and may also be familiar with platform guidelines for the use of content that is not their own. Potentially, students bring with them a broad, working knowledge of copyright from the perspective of an author/artist or that of a YouTube consumer. When the most popular YouTubers are blocked for copyright infringement, it's often big news discussed on their channel. Librarians can leverage this kind of basic knowledge to discuss concepts of fair use, permissions, the ethical use of images, text, and audio, and open access as these pertain to the students' intellectual and creative work.

At IWU, students are actively encouraged and mentored to pursue undergraduate research and independent study. A small percentage of students are eligible to pursue honors research, in which they embark on a 12–18 month independent project mentored by a faculty member. Other students pursue semester-long independent study or internships which carry with them an expectation of a cumulative project. Senior seminars, which function as capstone experiences for some majors, also feature deep research and writing; and some faculty members nominate student work to be included in the repository. IWU has a history of supporting undergraduate journals, and there are currently five such journals hosted on IWU's institutional repository, for political science (*Res Publica*), history (*Constructing History*), economics (*Park Place Economist, Undergraduate Economic Review*), and our Phi Beta Kappa chapter (*CrissCross*).[6] These journals are sponsored by departments, but the editorial work of peer review and selection is all done by students. Another long-standing tradition is IWU's John Wesley Powell Undergraduate Research Conference, which began in 1990 as a two-hour event with poster presentations from the sciences and social sciences. This conference has since expanded to a day-long event that spans all majors and programs, and it features poster and oral presentations, an art gallery presentation, musical performances of original student compositions, a keynote speaker, and the presentation of the Phi Beta Kappa Liberal Arts Scholar Award. The event is the unofficial kickoff to Commencement and is attended by students, faculty, staff, members of the board of trustees, parents, and prospective students and their families. Each of the venues described in this section provides students with the opportunity to share their work through our repository, which often brings up questions of copyright and permissions to use other scholars' work.

Our methods of outreach are highly variable and customized to the audience, but our message is consistently focused on how to share work ethically and judiciously. Each venue discussed above has a different mix of students, faculty, and administration involved and invested in the final products. Our honors program is administered through our associate provost's office, but the different departments often have their own traditions, expectations, and boundaries for sharing student work. For example, our Psychology Department has a long-standing history of students working in faculty members' labs, contributing to their research as well as running their own related research projects for the honors program. Typically, faculty members ask that students place an embargo on their honors theses until after the faculty publish their own work. Honors students from the English Department usually choose only to have metadata from their honors project in our repository, so they can pursue publication of their creative work after they graduate. Other departments are more liberal in their approach, such as the Economics Department, which encourages the sharing of students' honors work.

These choices carry over into how students share their research at the John Wesley Powell Undergraduate Research Conference. Though not all students who present at the conference are Honors students, some do not elect to deposit their work in the online conference archive because it's closely related to ongoing faculty research, or because the student's research is not yet complete. Disciplinary conventions and faculty members' understanding of open content definitely come into play in students' decision-making here. However, faculty do welcome the scholarly communications librarian into their classrooms and seminars to discuss with their students the benefits and consequences of sharing the results of their research openly. The Biology Department, for example, recently met with the scholarly communications librarian to put a process in place for the department to nominate and select which posters from the department should be included in the conference archive. This is a promising development, and one that could be emulated in different departments on campus. The benefit to departments is a presentation of the highest-quality work; the benefit to students is having an incentive to produce high-quality work, and then to be able to say it was selected from all the posters presented at the conference for inclusion in the repository. In general, however, discussions about what can and should be shared openly online need to start at the beginning of the research process, not at the end.

Our undergraduate research journals are sponsored by departments and have a long history of open access, but educating student-publishers about their author rights is relatively new. The scholarly communications librarian works most closely with the two economics journals, which are staffed by senior students who are selected by the faculty. The faculty who teach that department's senior seminar have invited the librarian into the course to present on open access, its impact on scholarly publishing, and the economics of publishing. The instruction session also serves as an overview of the students' responsibilities as peer reviewers for the journals, with an introduction to the reviewing platform and evaluative criteria. The scholarly communications librarian also serves as technical advisor to the journals sponsored by the Political Science and History departments and the IWU chapter of Phi Beta Kappa, assisting with the publishing platform.

Our education efforts attempt to cover a variety of concepts while respecting the different approaches to sharing research across the disciplines. While open is becoming more well-known in general, oftentimes individual faculty do not know where to start, or how. Discussions with students are often teachable moments for faculty and can lend themselves to further discussions beyond the class session. Challenges arise when the student's work is tied closely to a faculty member's research agenda and publication plans, when the product is a creative work, or when the faculty member is unsupportive or lacks knowledge of open sharing methods. Faculty members often express concerns over the possible plagiarism of openly shared work. This is an excellent opportunity to explain the risks and benefits of open access, and how sharing a project openly online is a point of registration, whereby students can establish their scholarly identity and intellectual ownership of their original, faculty-vetted works. There are also growing concerns and specific examples of bad actors' predatory behaviors on undergraduates in the scholarly publishing landscape. Again, this is an excellent opportunity not only to teach "caveat scholar,"[7] but also to encourage students to reach out to their scholarly networks—their faculty mentors, advisors, and librarians—to help them evaluate an offered publication opportunity.

CHALLENGES AND OPPORTUNITIES

There are significant global challenges for the small liberal arts institution with regard to copyright support services. Generally, university legal counsel is a contract position; there is no team of lawyers to go to for a risk analysis or for feedback on copyright issues. Designating a university copyright officer (UCO) is one way to provide educated assistance; however, copyright education is often expensive and may be out of reach for smaller institutions. Developing expertise with copyright and intellectual property takes time, both to build knowledge and experience with the variety of questions that arise in teaching and research, and to build word-of-mouth advertising for the expertise on campus. Another challenge for the copyright officer is working with other administrators who want to freely use content without seeking permission or who override the advice of the UCO, which can set up difficult working relationships. Furthermore, though we try to cover as much ground as possible with our educative efforts, a question we constantly ask is whether we are addressing the right groups at the right time. Honors projects, undergraduate journals, and our undergraduate research conference usually conclude at the end of the spring semester, which is a near-impossible time to engage in a series of thoughtful discussions about copyright, open access, and sharing of work.

However, there are opportunities to expand the reach of our copyright and open access education. Our General Education program is undergoing a deep and broad revision process, which may present us with a chance to reframe how we deliver information literacy instruction to include copyright as an integrated part of sessions instead of an additional piece. Specifically, we need to clarify our library faculty members' roles as experts on copyright as a matter of the ethical use of information, as a mechanism to serve authors and creators, and also as an opportunity to critically examine different applications of copyright in different areas that may or may not be consumer-friendly, such as the entertainment industry.

Another opportunity is our recent addition of the Illinois Small Business Development Center (SBDC) and the addition of both a new minor and a new interdisciplinary program: our Business Department started a minor in entrepreneurship; and the School of Art and the Physics and Business departments created a design, entrepreneurship, and technology major. The UCO and the scholarly communications librarian have already taken part in discussions within the SBDC and with members of each department about how to best protect the copyrights of students who design prototypes or other products as part of internships, practicums, or coursework. With the growth of entrepreneurship programs nationwide, copyright and intellectual property will be an increasingly important area of instruction and collaboration in the future between faculty, librarians, and students. Clarity in any policy and how the policy is applied will be vital to these programs and their students.

Finally, IWU is developing a Signature Experience program, dedicated to providing students with a culminating experience through which they apply the skills, outlooks, and intellectual capacity earned while studying at IWU. Currently, the traditional final product of these high-impact experiences is a paper, but there are faculty who are interested in students producing more creative work informed by scholarly practices, such as videos, multimodal projects, and online portfolios that are comprised of a combination of student work (e.g., papers, photographs, videos, etc.). Copyright education will be a vital piece of our contribution to the Signature Experience, and an excellent opportunity to establish a program of assessable educative moments for students and faculty alike.

The landscape of copyright education, outreach, and policy at a small liberal arts college is multifaceted, requiring not only professional development and an awareness of federal policy, but also an agile and flexible mindset in order to provide guidance to different users and different contexts. Balancing the needs of faculty, students, and administrators with best practices for scholarly publications, media, and the products of the institution can be challenging and necessitates maintaining strong connections with the network of copyright-savvy librarians within academic librarianship. While the quantity of copyright questions we receive may not equal our counterparts at research institutions, the scope of the examples we have presented indicates that teachable moments for copyright education are abundant no matter what the size of the institution is.

NOTES

1. Illinois Wesleyan University, "Intellectual Property Policy," chapter VI, part K, https://www.iwu.edu/provost/faculty-handbook.pdf.
2. There are a number of copyright blogs and e-mail lists that support continuing education for all formats. The Copyright Society of the USA maintains a list of blogs at https://www.csusa.org/page/LinksBlogs. Other e-mail lists that discuss copyright issues and provide guidance include SCHOLCOMM from the Association of College and Research Libraries (www.ala.org/acrl/issues/scholcomm/scholcommdiscussion); Reddit-Copyright; and LEH-Letter from Lesley Ellen Harris, a commercial copyright continuing education site that also provides some free resources. Many research institutions maintain robust copyright websites that offer a number of tools and links to resources.
3. Creative Commons, https://creativecommons.org/.
4. U.S. Copyright Office, "Fair Use Index," https://www.copyright.gov/fair-use/.
5. Copyright Alliance, https://copyrightalliance.org/ca_faq_post/rights-copyright-owners-ata/
6. Illinois Wesleyan University, "Student Journals," 2018, https://digitalcommons.iwu.edu/peer_review_list.html.
7. Curtis A. Olson, "Caveat Scholar: On the Growth of Predatory Publishing," *Journal of Continuing Education in the Health Professions* 37 (winter 2017): 1–2.

CARLA MYERS

9

Coaching up the Chain of Command

THE PAST TEN YEARS HAVE SEEN AN INCREASING NUMBER OF academic libraries looking to hire individuals who have knowledge of U.S. copyright law and experience in addressing library copyright issues. This fact is illustrated by research conducted by Kawooya, Veverka, and Lipinski (2015) that found that, between August 2006 and April 2013, of the 2,799 job advertisements posted to the American Library Association's JobLIST, 264 (9.4 percent) of them "mentioned 'copyright' in the title or text of the job advertisement . . . and 16 were copyright officer/manager type positions."[1] As academic library deans and directors often direct and approve the development of new librarian positions or the revision of responsibilities of existing positions, the growth of job advertisements requiring copyright knowledge indicates that library administrators recognize the need to have individuals on staff who can help address copyright issues. The work of copyright librarians is not usually limited to just addressing library copyright issues; most also assist other members of the campus community, including faculty, staff, students, and campus administrators, with copyright questions. Copyright librarians often answer specific types of questions for each of these audiences. Faculty and students frequently ask questions that relate to their own individual uses of works; for example, how third-party works can be used in the classroom, how these materials can be incorporated into new works that faculty and students are creating, or about the rights they possess under the law as the creators of copyrightable works. Library and campus administrators will sometimes ask these questions as well, but frequently they are focused on the larger issues of copyright policy development, the promotion and enforcement of these policies, and how best to mitigate the risk of claims of copyright infringement against the library or the academic institution. In this case study, I will outline the challenges a copyright librarian may face when helping library and campus administrators navigate copyright compliance, provide tips and best practices for overcoming these challenges, and make recommendations for building a network within institutions and across the profession to help identify and resolve copyright issues.

CHALLENGES

Serving as a copyright librarian can be a rewarding yet challenging experience. Some of the challenges encountered are created by the administrative structure of libraries and academic institutions themselves, but library and campus administrators are ideally poised to help copyright librarians respond to and overcome them.

CHALLENGE 1
Becoming a Copyright Librarian

While some librarians train for and actively seek employment as copyright librarians, frequently copyright librarian responsibilities are added on to an existing librarian position or incorporated into newly developed or revised positions. When a library administrator is looking to incorporate these responsibilities into a current position, they can sometimes find a staff member with a genuine interest in copyright law who will volunteer to take them on. However, it is also possible for a library administrator to walk into the office of a librarian and say "I'd like you to become our library's copyright expert." In these situations, a librarian with minimal or no prior knowledge of US copyright law may find themselves in the position of having to provide copyright information to their colleagues and members of the campus community.

CHALLENGE 2
Navigating Institutional Practices
in Policy Development

Though it is not often openly talked about, most academic institutions have their own "way of doing things," which can impact the work a copyright librarian is looking to do. For example, at some institutions proposals for new policies and practices must travel up the chain of command in certain ways, while at other institutions staff can go directly to their dean, director, or department head with these proposals. At some institutions, policy development occurs quickly and is done mostly within the department. At others, the development of new policies and procedures takes many, many months and involves obtaining feedback from multiple departments and administrative levels before approval. At some institutions, the decision-making power regarding the interpretation and application of policies and practices that have some legal risk involved lies with administrators only, while at other institutions the front-line staff are empowered to make these decisions. To be successful, a copyright librarian must identify how institutional practices influence the development of new policies and practices, and the best ways to navigate within this system.

CHALLENGE 3
Risk-Averse Institutions

Some library and campus administrators will be hesitant to sign off on new policies and practices that take advantage of the exceptions found in U.S. copyright law, fearing that copyright infringement lawsuits may be brought against the institution. Their fear is not unfounded, since lawsuits are expensive, time-consuming, and stressful for all involved. In these situations, a copyright librarian will need to be prepared to advocate for how a balance can be struck between the rights granted to the creators of copyrightable works under U.S. copyright law and the exceptions provided in the law for users, and be ready to make recommendations regarding risk management in an effort to help allay those concerns.

CHALLENGE 4
Avoidance of the Law

Alternately, a problem that copyright librarians may encounter is administrators who choose to ignore or avoid the law, thinking that ignorance of the law negates responsibility, that addressing copyright issues is not a priority, or who may be hesitant to change the scope of services that patrons or students are accustomed to receiving even if those services are not compliant with the law. In these situations, copyright librarians may need to take extra time and care with administrators to help mitigate the risk of claims of copyright infringement against the institution.

WHAT'S A COPYRIGHT LIBRARIAN TO DO?

Many of these challenges can be overcome when copyright librarians work closely with library and campus administrators to address copyright issues on campus in a proactive manner. In these situations, the copyright librarian will likely find they are the subject-matter expert in the room and are coaching their supervisor, library administrators, and senior members of the academic institution's administrative team on best practices for complying with the law. With preparation and a collaborative attitude, copyright librarians can be well-prepared to undertake these responsibilities, help administrators understand the law, and establish policies and practices that support the educational mission of the library and academic institution while still working within the scope and intent of the law.

STEP 1

Becoming a Copyright Librarian Starts with Learning about the Law

In a 2017 interview Peter Jaszi, a retired law professor and faculty director of the Glushko-Samuelson Intellectual Property Clinic, provided sound advice for librarians who are assigned copyright responsibilities by an administrator. Instead of telling the administrator, "No, I will not do this," he recommends:

> Turn . . . to whoever [asked you to take on these responsibilities] and say, "Look, I'll do this. I'm a team player, but I need training." Because there are an awful lot of opportunities for training that are available. An awful lot of seminars and sessions, especially those that are run by professional organizations, that librarians can take advantage of. And I would urge anyone . . . to say "Send me to the ALA [American Library Association] programs, the ARL [Association of Research Libraries] programs, the ACRL [Association of College and Research Libraries] programs that deal with [copyright] issues. Let me learn from people who know."[2]

Since library administrators oversee the budget and can be involved in setting work schedules and establishing priorities, an opportunity exists for the newly minted copyright librarian to approach her dean or director to establish prioritized time in her schedule to participate in training opportunities, with financial support from the institution to do so. At a minimum, this training can involve acquiring quality treatises on U.S. copyright law that can be incorporated into the library's collection and serve as reference resources for the library staff and members of the academic institution. This should be an easy request for administrators to grant, since it fits within the scope of a library's collection development practices. These titles should include the book you are currently reading, and should also include, but are not limited to:

> Kenneth D. Crews, *Copyright Law for Librarians and Educators: Creative Strategies and Practical Solutions,* 4th ed. (Chicago: American Library Association, 2018).

Donna L. Ferullo, *Managing Copyright in Higher Education: A Guidebook* (Lanham, MD: Rowman and Littlefield, 2014).

Mary LaFrance, *Copyright Law in a Nutshell,* 3rd ed. (St. Paul, MN: West Academic, 2017).

Tomas A. Lipinski, *The Complete Copyright Liability Handbook for Librarians and Educators* (New York: Neal-Schuman, 2005).

The training should also involve funding for the new copyright librarian to travel to conferences, symposiums, and workshops where qualified, knowledgeable instructors provide training on library and campus copyright issues. These opportunities give the copyright librarian an opportunity to engage with session instructors, as well as meet other copyright librarians and begin to build a network of peers who have similar job responsibilities. In his 2017 interview, Peter Jaszi encouraged copyright librarians to network, stating, "there are more and more supporting networks for people who are doing copyright jobs in various libraries to take advantage of, and [copyright librarians] really should do that. [They] will learn an enormous amount from [their] peers and from the opportunity to be in touch with [their] peers."[3]

If budget restrictions or staffing issues (or both) do not allow a new copyright librarian to travel for training in their first year, then they should seek permission from their dean or director to prioritize time in their schedule to participate in high-quality online programs that explore library copyright issues. Many of these programs are free of charge. Three of them are the following:

CopyrightX

http://copyx.org/#

This is an online, twelve-week course that "explores the current law of copyright; the impact of that law on art, entertainment, and industry; and the ongoing debates concerning how the law should be reformed."[4]

Copyright for Educators & Librarians

https://www.coursera.org/learn/copyright-for-education

This online course is "designed to provide a basic introduction to U.S. copyright law and . . . provide participants with a practical framework for analyzing copyright issues that they encounter in their professional work."[5]

CopyTalk Webinars

www.ala.org/advocacy/pp/pub/copytalk

These monthly webinars, sponsored by the ALA's Washington Office, explore "specific copyright topics that include orphan works, mass digitization, international copyright developments, pending and recent copyright court cases, the copyright implications of new technologies, and more."[6]

Access to training opportunities and resources should not be limited to just the first few months or years of a new copyright librarian's tenure. Because the copyright law can be changed or interpretations of the law can be impacted by new court decisions, library administrators should provide support for copyright librarians to engage in continuing education opportunities throughout their career.

STEP 2
Developing a Game Plan for Providing Copyright Services

The copyright librarian will need to work closely with their dean or director in order to determine the scope of their responsibilities. Questions to discuss include what services the copyright librarian will provide, how much of their time will be spent providing copyright services, and the decision-making power that will be granted to them when developing copyright policies and best practices for the library and the campus community. Emilie Regina Algenio's 2018 article "Making the Transition as the New Copyright Librarian," published in the *Journal of Copyright in Education and Librarianship*,[7] provides tips and best practices for new copyright librarians to follow in undertaking their responsibilities. New copyright librarians should suggest to their administrator that he read this article, and find time to meet with them on a regular basis in order to identify which practices and services identified in the article are a good fit for their institution and how the library can best provide support as the new copyright librarian begins to establish a copyright education program.

STEP 3
Identify Allies on Campus

In this situation, "allies" will be the people on campus or within the copyright librarian's college or university system who can help them learn about the law, promote compliance with the law, assist them in navigating institutional practices when looking to develop new copyright policies and best practices, and help support them in their work. The library's dean or director will ideally be a copyright librarian's greatest source of support, but they should not be their only source of support. Copyright librarians should work closely with administrators in their library in order to identify potential allies across campus. These allies may include but are not limited to the following.

Attorneys from the Office of General Counsel

Most institutions of higher education have an office of general counsel staffed by attorneys who "[supervise] litigation involving the [institution] and [provide] a wide range of legal services in the areas of employment and benefits, immigration, contracts, student affairs, real estate, and intellectual property."[8] While some copyright librarians, especially those without law degrees, may be hesitant to seek out and work with the institution's legal counsel, fearing they don't have the credentials or knowledge needed to converse with someone with a law degree, this should not be the case. In the same way that many patrons, colleagues, and members of the campus community are eager to engage with the copyright librarian, it is likely that the attorneys in the office of general counsel will be eager to do so as well for a variety of reasons. While many campus attorneys realize that copyright issues arise frequently in academia and need to be addressed, they may not be able to give them the same priority as some of the other legal issues facing the institution, such as pending lawsuits. As such, most campus attorneys will welcome the opportunity to work with a knowledgeable and competent copyright librarian who can serve as the first point of contact for faculty, staff, and students who have copyright questions.

Copyright librarians should not be surprised to find that they are able to educate their campus attorneys about copyright law. Unless the attorney they are working with specialized in intellectual property law or has prior work experience in this field, it is likely that they may have only had a few weeks of instruction in copyright during an introductory course on intellectual property law that they took in law school. In these situations, copyright librarians and the institution's attorneys can form a mutual partnership through which the copyright librarian can help guide their institution's attorneys through the nuances of U.S. copyright law, and the campus attorneys can assist the copyright librarian with technical legal work (e.g., drafting legal documents, and reviewing contracts that include copyright clauses). When needed, the campus attorneys can also provide the librarian with legal advice regarding the development of campus copyright policies and best practices.

Deans, Directors, and Department Heads
from Other Campus Schools and Departments

The deans, directors, and department heads of the various schools and departments found around campus can also be useful allies. These administrators may have been asked copyright questions and, as a result, may understand the copyright issues that their staff and faculty struggle with. They can also advise the copyright librarian on policies and practices within their academic unit that are impacted by copyright, or they can help assemble a team from their unit to work with the copyright librarian when policies and practices need to be reviewed for compliance with the law. They can also invite the copyright librarian to attend a departmental meeting so that they can introduce themselves to the faculty and staff, speak for a few minutes about the services they provide, and distribute their contact information so that those with copyright questions can easily follow up with them. It will be especially important for the copyright librarian to establish a relationship with administrators in the department that oversees the institution's content management system (e.g. Canvas, Moodle, or Blackboard), with the administrators in the instructional design department, and with the manager of the campus copy shop. These are departments whose services will often involve the copying, distribution, and performance of copyrighted works. As such, building relationships with these department administrators will help ensure that the copyright librarian can be available to answer questions that staff in these departments have, and assist them in developing policies and best practices to help ensure that their work falls within the scope of the law.

Campus Administration

The campus provost or president will also play a key role in encouraging members of the campus community to comply with the law, and can provide the copyright librarian with the support needed when policies and best practices regarding copyright law are implemented campus-wide. If there are multiple branches or campuses within the institution, the copyright librarian should also reach out to the administrators on those campuses to establish relationships and help them address copyright issues.

PUTTING IT ALL TOGETHER

As stated previously, library and campus administrators will likely seek input from the copyright librarian in three key areas: (1) copyright policy development, (2) promoting compliance with the law among members of the library staff and campus community, and (3) mitigating the risk of claims of copyright infringement against the library and the academic institution.

Policy Development

Copyright librarians will likely find themselves invited or directed to consult with fellow staff members and others in the campus community to develop new policies and best practices for working through copyright issues. In its simplest form, this can be done by:

1. Helping to identify the copyright issue at hand (e.g., faculty looking to make and distribute copies of a copyrighted work such as articles and book chapters to students, or the library staff interested in giving public performances of the films in their collection for patrons).
2. Identifying the options available under U.S. copyright law that may apply to the situation (e.g., could the copying and distribution of the work be considered a fair use; was the DVD acquired with a public performance

license, could the film screening fall under the classroom exception found in subsection 110(1) of U.S. copyright law, or could permission be obtained for the screening?).

3. Drafting policies and best practice documents that are written in plain English and can help members of the campus community learn more about U.S. copyright law and make thoughtful and informed decisions on how to proceed in the aforementioned situations.

Here it will be especially important for the copyright librarian to consult with their library's administration to identify and work within any institutional practices that may affect policy development. For example, at some institutions it may be perfectly acceptable for the copyright librarian to propose new policies and best practices pertaining to U.S. copyright law within the library. However, when working with faculty and staff in other departments, proposals like these may need to go through specific committees within the department or through various individuals in order to be received and considered. A good library dean or director will have an understanding of how things work in various departments across campus and will likely have their own allies and contacts within those departments that they can use to help the copyright librarian succeed in getting these new initiatives implemented.

Another point of clarity that copyright librarians will need relates to who has the final decision-making authority when it comes to interpreting copyright policies and best practices. It will be critically important for those working on the front lines to know what authority they have when making determinations regarding the law; for example, making fair use decisions, digitizing works whose copyright status is unknown (orphan works), and providing recommendations and information to users regarding the law. If this decision-making ability lies with the front-line staff, then the copyright librarian can work with departments that operate under the copyright policies to provide training to these staff so they can make informed and thoughtful interpretations of the copyright policy and the law. If the staff are not empowered to make these decisions, then the copyright librarian must work with administrators to determine who will interpret copyright policy and have the final word on various copyright issues.

The tools and resources that can aid copyright librarians in policy development include:

Kevin L. Smith and William M. Cross, "Developing Copyright Policy: A Guide for Liberal Arts Colleges," Oberlin Group of Libraries, 2010, www.oberlingroup.org/developing-copyright-policy-guide-liberal -arts-colleges.

The "Institutional Policies" section of the Copyright Crash Course website, developed by Georgia Harper, http://guides.lib.utexas.edu/ copyright/instpolicy.

Promoting Compliance with the Law

Having sound copyright policies and practices in place that are based on the law is the first step in promoting copyright compliance on campus. Policy and practice documents should have the contact information for the copyright librarian placed on them prominently so that members of the campus community can easily make contact if they have questions. The copyright librarian should also speak with their campus administrator about prioritizing time in her schedule to offer workshops, brown-bag sessions, or other informational sessions through which members of the campus community can learn more about the copyright law. Here, too, relationships with other administrators across campus can play an important role because they can help facilitate communication between those who may be utilizing a copyright policy (e.g., a faculty member looking to post a reading to the content management system) and the copyright librarian. Alternatively, in the case of department-specific copyright policies, the administrator can invite the copyright librarian to provide educational sessions for those in the department who will be working under the policy.

Copyright librarians should not set out to be the "copyright police," and they should make sure that administrators are not portraying them as individuals who are looking to get staff, faculty, and students into trouble for reusing copyrighted works in teaching, learning, and the creation of new works. Instead, the copyright librarian should work with administrators in their library to market their services as a reference resource for members of the campus community. In the same way that subject specialists can help students, faculty, and staff identify, connect with, and use high-quality information in a particular subject area, so too should the copyright librarian be viewed as a facilitator for helping members of the campus community identify and use high-quality information about the law.

Risk Management

Most interactions that the copyright librarian will have with fellow staff members in the library and with students, faculty, and staff in other departments will be positive. There will be times, however, when individuals or groups will choose to ignore the advice of the copyright librarian or disregard copyright policy. In these situations, copyright librarians should prepare to stand their ground and advocate for what is right, but they should also find champions who can stand beside them and help remedy the situation. These champions will come from the campus allies the librarians have identified and could include the following ones.

The Library Dean or Director

Within the library, the dean or director will have the authority needed to address a situation where a colleague on staff is ignoring or disregarding the copyright librarian's recommendations on how to resolve a copyright issue. The dean or director will also likely have thoughts and recommendations on how best to proceed when the copyright librarian's advice regarding campus copyright issues, such as film screenings and classroom photocopying, is being ignored by members of the campus community. In the case of working with people from other departments, the dean or director may be able to work through administrative channels to resolve problematic situations, or put the copyright librarian in touch with someone in the department who can help ensure that copyright policies are followed.

Attorneys from the Office of General Counsel

In situations where the copyright librarian's advice and recommendations are being ignored, the campus attorneys can also step in and, if needed, mandate that the offending parties comply with the law, or possibly even suspend the infringing service until changes are made to bring it within the scope of the law. Copyright librarians who have worked in their field for some time will attest to the fact that some faculty and staff who disregard copyright policies and best practices will respond more readily when they are told "no" or "stop that!" by a campus attorney rather than by the copyright librarian.

Responding to Inquiries from Rights Holders

Mitigating the risks of copyright infringement will also involve working with identified allies to respond to inquiries from rights holders who are concerned that the reuse of their work by the library, students, faculty, or staff is infringing on their copyright. These inquiries may range from polite e-mails asking about the use of a third-party work by a member of the campus community, to a cease and desist letter demanding that the third-party work stop being used, to a lawsuit brought against the institution for copyright infringement. The copyright librarian should work with campus administrators and attorneys from the office of general counsel to determine how they will respond to these inquiries.

REMEMBERING THE MISSION

In every interaction, copyright librarians should seek to provide high-quality information about the law to members of the campus community and help mitigate legal risk for the institution. However, they should also strive to uphold the mission of their library and the larger educational institution, which usually involves providing access to information, helping to promote scholarly inquiry, and supporting the development and dissemination of new scholarly works. This mission actually aligns closely with the purpose of the copyright law as outlined in article 1, section 8, clause 8 of the U.S. Constitution, which aims to "promote the progress of science and useful arts, by securing for limited times to authors and inventors the exclusive right to their respective writings and discoveries." Balance can be achieved by respecting the rights the law grants to those who create copyrighted works while also advocating for the development of policies and practices that support the reuse of works within the scope of the exceptions found in U.S. copyright law. Library and campus administrators should be seen as allies, not adversaries, who can help copyright librarians achieve these goals, and the copyright librarian should value the role they can play in helping institutional leaders promote ethical applications of the law in their library and on campus.

BIBLIOGRAPHY

Algenio, Emilie Regina. "The Erasure of Language." *Journal of Copyright in Education and Librarianship* 2, no. 1 (2018): 1–24. doi: https://doi.org/10.17161/jcel.v2i1.6579.

American Library Association. "CopyTalk Webinars." June 27, 2018. www.ala.org/advocacy/pp/pub/copytalk.

CopyrightX. "CopyrightX Course Overview." http://copyx.org/course-overview/.

Jaszi, Peter, interview by Carla Myers, Tucker Taylor, and Andrew Wesolek. March 8, 2017, transcript.

Kawooya, Dick, Amber Veverka, and Tomas Lipinski. "The Copyright Librarian: A Study of Advertising Trends for the Period 2006–2013." *Journal of Academic Librarianship* 41 (2015): 341–49. doi: 10.1016/j.acalib.2015.02.011.

Miami University. "Office of General Counsel." http://miamioh.edu/about-miami/leadership/general-counsel/.

Smith, Kevin, Lisa A. Macklin, and Anne Gilliland. "Copyright for Educators and Librarians." Coursera. https://www.coursera.org/learn/copyright-for-education.

NOTES

1. Dick Kawooya, Amber Veverka, and Tomas Lipinski, "The Copyright Librarian: A Study of Advertising Trends for the Period 2006–2013," *Journal of Academic Librarianship* 41 (2015): 341–49, doi:10.1016/j.acalib.2015.02.011.
2. Peter Jaszi, in discussion with the author, Tucker Taylor, and Andrew Wesolek, March 2017.
3. Jaszi, in discussion with the author, March 2017.

4. CopyrightX, "CopyrightX Course Overview," http://copyx.org/course -overview/.

5. Kevin Smith, Lisa A. Macklin, and Anne Gilliland, "Copyright for Educators and Librarians," Coursera, https://www.coursera.org/learn/ copyright-for-education.

6. American Library Association, "CopyTalk Webinars," June 27, 2018, www.ala .org/advocacy/pp/pub/copytalk.

7. Emilie Regina Algenio, "Making the Transition as the New Copyright Librarian," *Journal of Copyright in Education and Librarianship* 2, no. 1 (2018): 1–24, doi:https://doi.org/10.17161/jcel.v2i1.6579.

8. Miami University, "Office of General Counsel," http://miamioh.edu/about -miami/leadership/general-counsel/.

10

A Five-Year Review of a "Legal Issues for Librarians" Course

A GAP IN LIS INSTRUCTION

In the spring of 2012, the University of North Carolina at Chapel Hill's School of Information and Library Science (UNC SILS) debuted a new course. The topic—"Legal Issues for Librarians"—had never been offered at UNC SILS before and was rarely offered in library and information science (LIS) programs anywhere in North America. The course was aligned with the American Library Association's Core Competencies, which indicate that LIS graduates "should know and, where appropriate, be able to employ . . . the legal framework within which libraries and information agencies operate. That framework includes laws relating to copyright, privacy, freedom of expression, equal rights (e.g., the Americans with Disabilities Act), and intellectual property."[1] Despite this clear language, the state of legal education for librarians when the course was being designed in 2011 was—and remains in 2018[2]—"rare, patchwork, and elective."[3]

Because the new course filled this important gap, LIS students quickly enrolled and the course was an immediate hit, receiving high marks from student evaluations, which indicated that the course made complex issues engaging and made students feel better prepared to navigate legal issues once they had finished their program and moved into the profession. In light of this success, the course was regularized and offered on a recurring basis each subsequent spring.

After five years, it seems appropriate to review and take stock. How have student evaluations of this course trended over the subsequent half-decade? How have former students actually experienced legal issues in their careers? Do they still feel, with the benefit of hindsight and several years on the job, that the course was useful for them and was worth the time for new students who are currently preparing for their own careers?

To help answer these questions, this chapter offers an overview of the course and an evaluation of its effectiveness for working librarians. It presents a review of five years of course evaluations, as well as the results of a survey sent to every student who completed the course. By presenting both the initial evaluations from students who had just completed the course as well as their review after working in the field for several years, this chapter will offer insights into one model for successful copyright education, as well as a review of what aspects of the course seemed most useful to students at different stages of their careers.

THE COURSE
Legal Issues for Librarians

"Legal Issues for Librarians" was offered as a response to a petition by current students, who felt that they would benefit from an introduction to these topics. Initially, the new course was co-taught by Will Cross, a recent UNC SILS and law school graduate, and Kevin Smith, the director of copyright and scholarly communication at Duke University. The course offered an overview of legal research, sources, and terminology, as well as deep dives into the legal topics that are most relevant to librarianship. The first month of the course focused on copyright and licensing, with an emphasis on formalities, exceptions like fair use, and copyright in library collections. The course then turned to free expression, privacy, and intellectual freedom. Finally, the course covered a set of professional issues such as employment law, safety, and equality of access.

The course was built around hands-on engagement with legal materials like statutes and case law, as well as scholarship that connects legal issues with library practice. Weekly three-hour meetings began with a high-level discussion of the principles at issue and the lived experiences of students, and then turned to active discussion of legal rules as applied to library work. The second half of the course meetings was devoted to hands-on work such as reviewing contracts, analyzing specific cases, and evaluating job descriptions for potential legal problems. Course assignments were built around case analysis through a customized version of the standard IRAC method of case briefing that is familiar to most law students.[4] The IRAC (Issue, Rule, Analysis, Conclusion) method asks students to review a case and write up a brief that outlines the *issues* considered by the court, the *rule* applied by that court, the way the court used that rule to *analyze* the issue, and finally the *conclusion* reached by the court. The course also asked students to add a fifth section detailing their personal impressions of the case and their understanding of how the case might impact librarianship. By having students walk through the modified IRAC process, the assignment was designed to offer scaffolding for the often-new experience of reading legal documents, as well as prepare them to discuss specific aspects of the case and the principles it introduced. Final assignments in the initial course involved developing a white paper or a set of guidelines for addressing a current legal challenge in a particular type of library (academic, public, school, etc.) as identified by each student, or by a group of students working together.

Initially offered as a Special Topics course, "Legal Issues for Librarians" was regularized into a standard course and has been taught each spring from 2012 through 2017. In that half-decade the course has evolved in several ways, adding more case analysis, refining the final assignment, and modifying topical coverage based on new developments in the law and practice of librarianship. After the fourth year, Smith stepped away from the course and Anne Gilliland, UNC's scholarly communications officer, joined Cross as co-instructor.

Course Evaluations

A review of course evaluations across those five years reveals several common threads. Students almost uniformly enjoyed and appreciated the course, with a median score of "strongly agree" that the course was excellent, that the instructors were effective, and that students learned a great deal from the course.

Students also praised the assigned readings, the topics covered, and the mixture of discussion and hands-on work. Students particularly appreciated the IRAC assignment, which familiarized them with materials that had previously seemed intimidatingly technical or mysterious. They also appreciated the way the IRAC method served as a "steppingstone" to subsequent assignments. In some semesters, an annotated bibliography was also assigned, and this was also rated highly.

Students' views on the final assignment were more mixed. They did generally appreciate the "freedom to explore a topic of our choice, as well as a topic that is applicable to our future career interests," but they often struggled with the format. Initially charged to work individually and then present to the class, some students felt that individual work was artificial and that watching so many presentations was not the best use of class time. As one student wrote, "the policy and best practices assignment was incredibly valuable, but the process of writing it entirely on one's own does not mirror policy development in the real world, which would be an intensely collaborative experience."

In response, the final assignment was changed to a group project the following year, with an emphasis on bringing diverse stakeholders together, coalition-building, and compromise. Students still appreciated the hands-on work that was tailored to their interests and expected career paths, but (perhaps not surprisingly) they objected to working in groups. Subsequent iterations of the final assignment have continued to evolve to support tailored, practical projects that have better scaffolding, and students frequently praise the final assignment as the culmination of a course designed to prepare them for the day-to-day work of librarianship. As one student evaluation concluded, "I especially appreciate the emphasis on applying the course content to practical situations in which a librarian would be dealing with legal issues."

Based on student evaluations, this course appears to have been a great success. Students summarizing their experience at the end of the semester gave it high praise and specifically expressed appreciation for a course they felt had prepared them for practical library work. "No other classes address legal issues librarians will face in their careers, so this is a great background to have." What those evaluations cannot indicate, however, is whether those good feelings carried over into students' actual experiences on the job. Did the readings, discussions, and exercises actually prepare them to navigate legal issues in their practice, or did students leave with a false sense of confidence? Were there topics they didn't anticipate needing to understand that they encountered on the job? In order to better answer these questions, we asked them directly.

Methods

In order to understand students' perceptions of the quality of the course as it applied to professional library practice, those who had completed the course in the preceding five years were surveyed in fall 2017. In total, 101 students had completed the course in the past five years. Former students were surveyed using Qualtrics and were contacted directly by e-mail. Contact information was gathered from alumni records, which included several unresponsive or outdated e-mail addresses.

This survey employed the use of thirteen questions to collect data, capitalizing on the inherent advantage of survey research to uncover inferences in a population based on a small sample.[5] The questions were designed to elicit former students' current roles in the profession and their perception of the relevance of the course to those roles, as well as the utility of the course for current students. The survey used a series of Likert-type questions to rate the quality and utility of the course and specific assignments. The survey also offered a set of free text responses where former students could discuss their impressions and recommendations.

The surveys were sent via e-mail, although a handful (12) were returned due to an out-of-date e-mail address on file with the alumni office. Of the 89 former students who were contacted, 62 surveys were started and 55 were completed, for a response rate of 70 percent partial and 61 percent completed responses.

Results

Role and Relevance

The survey began with an overview of former students' current roles in and outside of librarianship (figure 10.1). A substantial majority of the respondents (65 percent) were employed as academic librarians, with another 15 percent working in a public library, and only 5 percent in a school library. Significantly, the second-largest group of respondents reported working outside of the traditional "big three" types of libraries. Respondents who listed their place of employment as "other" included digital scholarship staff, doctoral students, and librarians in the government, such as policy advisors in major federal agencies. Taken together, the survey revealed a heavy concentration in academic librarianship and related higher education fields such as law libraries, digital scholarship, and archives. Overall, roughly 75 percent of the respondents spend their work hours in higher education, in one form or another.

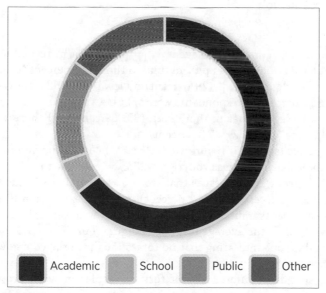

FIGURE 10.1
Career Path

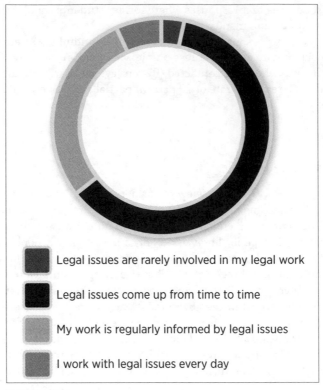

FIGURE 10.2

Legal Issues in Daily Work

As shown in figure 10.2, an even higher percentage of respondents indicated that legal issues "come up from time to time" (60 percent) or that their work "is regularly informed" (29 percent) by legal issues like copyright. The remaining 10 percent of respondents were split between those who are "rarely involved" with legal issues in their work (3.6 percent) and those who work with legal issues "every day" (7.3 percent).

The specific legal topic (figure 10.3) that came up most often for respondents in their daily work was copyright (25.8 percent), with privacy not far behind (22 percent). Other issues that arose for respondents included licensing (16 percent), accessibility (14 percent), and free expression (8 percent). Overall, respondents indicated that the topics covered were relevant to their current work, with the average response tagging four of the listed topics as relevant and no one indicating that no topics taught in the course were relevant to their work.

The respondents offered almost forty examples of work projects that were informed by the issues covered in the course. These ranged from standard consultations and policy-making to boutique digital scholarship projects.

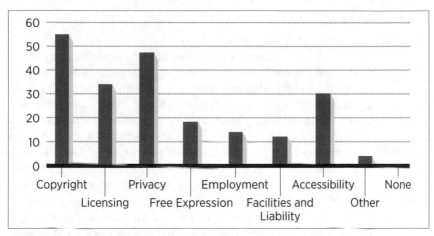

FIGURE 10.3
Legal Topics in Daily Work

Several respondents indicated that the training they received in their course prepared them to be the "de facto copyright guru for campus" even when their formal job title did not include copyright. Particularly for librarians working at smaller institutions, community colleges, and for-profit institutions, legal issues like copyright were "omnipresent" in student projects, scholarly works, and patron interactions.

In addition to core copyright issues, many respondents made it clear that the legal issues they faced in their professional lives cut across the topics discussed in the course. The most common example offered was digitization, which implicated copyright, but also privacy, licensing, and a host of other related issues. Similarly, respondents pointed to their professional role in understanding and interpreting licenses and terms of service, which required a knowledge of copyright, contracts, and privacy, as well as the implications of boilerplate terms such as jurisdiction and indemnification clauses.

This recognition that copyright knowledge cannot exist in a vacuum extended to the respondents' recognizing the value of a "general awareness of [legal] issues" so they could understand existing and emerging issues across campus and "be able to converse with colleagues in faculty and administration about them in an informed manner." Likewise, respondents also valued "the critical thinking skills and analysis that we practiced in the class." These values, which were often framed as "thinking like a lawyer," play a critical role in the way the course prepared students to evaluate complex, nuanced issues like fair use, and point to the larger value of holistic legal education that trains librarians to engage with legal issues and legal approaches writ large. As discussed below, this holistic approach, which emphasizes critical thinking and comfort with legal materials and practices, is at the heart of the respondents' evaluation of the course assignments.

The IRAC Assignment

The first assignment students evaluated was the IRAC assignment, which asked students to read a legal case, summarize it, and then offer their analysis of the case's legal implications, as well as practical takeaways for working librarians. Figure 10.4 shows that respondents had high marks for the IRAC assignment. On a Likert-type scale of 1–5, roughly 75 percent of former students rated the assignment highly as a 4 or 5. Conversely, only 7 percent rated it a disapproving 1 or 2. While some students acknowledged a hazy memory of specific assignments from a course they had taken four or five years ago, most comments about the assignment were positive, and many were effusive.

Many former students mentioned the value of the IRAC assignment as a way to "make legal materials less intimidating, particularly through the review of multiple cases." One student noted that "this was a tough assignment, but it made me realize I could read a legal case and explain its significance." The IRAC technique was singled out as "a great way of breaking down something that felt intimidating into manageable components." Former students appreciated that the specific cases selected often included engaging fact patterns, as well as popular topics such as appropriation art (*Cariou v. Prince*) and Harry Potter fan works (*Warner Bros. Entertainment, Inc. and J. K. Rowling v. RDR Books*). One student summed up the experience by describing the IRAC assignment as "my favorite writing assignment in graduate school."

Former students particularly noted the value of the IRAC assignment as a way to introduce them to a new type of writing. As one noted, "cases are unlike academic papers and were daunting until we practiced repeatedly." With that practice under their belt, however, students gained confidence in the forms

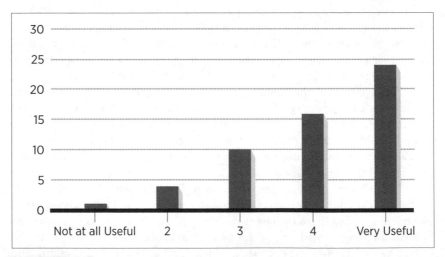

FIGURE 10.4
IRAC Assignment

and conventions of legal writing. One former student offered an anecdote about their own "confidence in legal issues and my ability to figure out things on my own," noting a situation where they worked with law students at a prestigious program and were recognized for their comfort with legal materials. "I think that interactions like this have empowered me to try to learn more about legal issues rather be intimidated by them."

The Final Assignment

Students also appreciated the final assignment (figure 10.5). Just under 70 percent of former students rated it a 4 or 5 on a five-point Likert-type scale, and only a single former student gave the assignment a 1 or 2. Because the final assignment changed somewhat over the five years, the students' experiences varied based on which semester they took the course. At the same time, former students from every semester seemed to appreciate the fact that the assignment was constantly updated based on previous feedback and was tailored to the size of the course in a given semester.

While some students echoed the frustration with group work that had been expressed in the initial evaluations of the course, the consensus among former students who responded was that the final assignment was generally helpful because it had clear practical applications to their work. Several former students mentioned the value of simply raising their awareness of policy documents and the issues that go into creating a policy.

Those former students who had any sort of policy role in their current job naturally valued the final assignment. As one wrote, "I am adept at analyzing policy documents rather than simply accepting them. This assignment

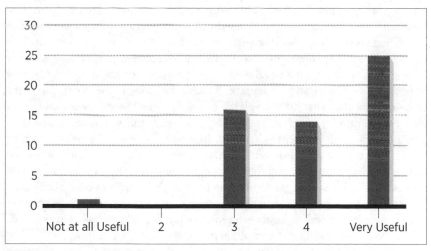

FIGURE 10.5
Final Assignment

prepared me to have legal justifications for policies I would propose as a department head." Even those without an explicit policy role appreciated the way the assignment had empowered them to critique and ask for changes in policies.

Particularly for students who may have felt unprepared to suggest policy changes in their current position, the credibility of the course loomed large. One student noted that, "in altering policies at my current job I frequently mention the phrase 'In my legal studies class taught by a real lawyer . . .' None of my other coworkers had the option for such a class, and as the youngest member of the staff I appreciate the social weight it gives my opinions on policy."

Overall, students enjoyed the opportunity to explore issues that felt relevant to their career, even if their career had taken an unexpected path. The core value that many students discovered on the job was in understanding "how a specific legal issue can be approached from multiple perspectives and utilize different kinds of resources." As one former student noted, "This may have been the single most helpful assignment in library school in terms of how I do research and write in my current work . . . This assignment gave me a rubric for how to present my research in a concise way, and how to include clear, practical recommendations for my organization."

Gaps

While students spoke highly of the topics covered by the course, the survey did ask for help identifying gaps in its coverage, and a few respondents did offer some suggestions. Copyright was specifically mentioned, but in a variety of contexts. While many students felt that "copyright and licensing were well covered," several asked for more coverage, especially focusing on copyright and vendor agreements, library obligations when responding to platforms like ResearchGate, and similar questions about third-party liability. On the other hand, one student expressed frustration that the course was "so overwhelmingly dominated by copyright" that it affected the coverage of other topics.

Several students also suggested expanding the coverage of neighboring issues such as patent and trademark. Specific facilities issues were also mentioned, particularly delicate or volatile issues such as the use of computers to view pornographic materials, as well as the general ability to remove and trespass patrons. A few students also suggested adding topics like accessibility or ethics, which were added in subsequent semesters after they had completed the course. Students also suggested timely topics that they wished had been more thoroughly covered, particularly in light of the "current political climate." Topics like equal protection and immigration under the current administration were suggested, as well as legal requirements for reporting sexual harassment, "given what is happening on campus across the country right now."

One theme struck by several students was their recognition that although they felt prepared, they couldn't be sure that there weren't gaps in the course that they were not aware of. As one student noted, "This course was actually fairly comprehensive, but also you don't know what you don't know. There haven't been any legal issues I've come across where I felt completely at a loss." Similarly, several former students noted that no course can completely prepare them for every legal issue that may arise in librarianship, especially since their careers are likely to take many forms: "I would have personally benefited from instruction that covers things in my assigned field, but there is no way to know that ahead of time." Instead, students appreciated the general grounding and asked for more guidance on how to discover new sources and keep up to speed on evolving topics. One went further, suggesting that "a post-grad refresher course would be beneficial to those who, like myself, have encountered course topics and issues but have had a few years since graduation."

Overall Quality

Overall, students affirmed their initial perceptions that they had been well-prepared for engaging with legal issues in their careers by the course (figure 10.6). More than 90 percent of students rated themselves as a 4 or 5 on a five-point Likert-type scale rating their level of preparedness to "identify the major legal issues facing librarians and the legal regulations that govern them." More than 60 percent similarly rated their ability to "locate and employ reliable sources of legal information to support practice and guide institutional decision-making in a changing legal environment," to "read and analyze primary legal materials such as statutes and case law," and to "create policy to guide best practice in

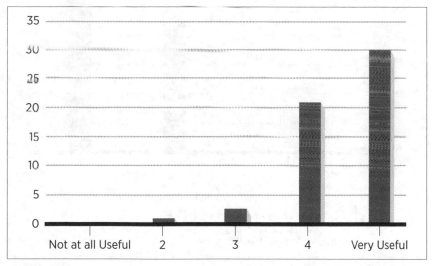

FIGURE 10.6
Preparedness

[their] chosen field." No former student rated themself as unprepared for any of these areas, and less than 10 percent (5 students) ranked themselves below a 3 of 5 points in any area.

Similarly, more than 90 percent of former students indicated that they found the class "very useful," and only one student rated it below a 3 of 5 points (figure 10.7). Given these responses, it is not surprising that nearly every former student (98 percent) indicated that they would recommend the course to any current LIS student, regardless of what area of librarianship they expect to work in. More striking, a majority of former students (54.5 percent) went further, and indicated that they felt this course should be required for graduation from an LIS program.

Speaking to their overall impressions of the course, students reiterated their enjoyment of it and affirmed the value of the course for LIS professionals. Many echoed the sentiment that "this course was extremely relevant and valuable to me in my professional life—it covered many of the legal issues I encounter on a daily basis." From music librarians to middle-school media specialists, former students emphasized the value of the course across a host of diverse LIS careers. They also indicated that the materials covered in the course came up regularly in their professional practice. As one noted, "I refer

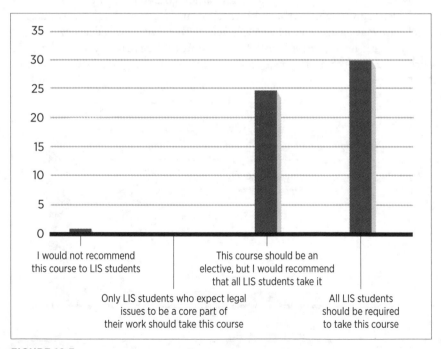

FIGURE 10.7
Utility

to information that I learned in this course on a weekly, sometimes daily basis (I often find myself wanting to correct some of my colleagues about their interpretation of fair use!)."

Former students repeatedly returned to the idea that the course was not only useful, but also empowering. By "familiariz[ing them] with the stylized language used in legal documents," the course prepared students to answer questions, but also to move beyond "living in fear" so they could "become active in areas, such as policy-making, as methods of advocating for our profession as well as for our patrons." One student summed up this sense of empowerment in detail:

> I think this course was useful because it gave me a general awareness of some of the most common legal issues related to libraries (and archives). I am not an expert on any one issue, and I don't need to be, but I do feel like I have a general understanding of the intellectual debates and practical implications surrounding a variety of issues. I feel confident discussing them with colleagues and well-prepared to investigate on my own when I need more information about a particular topic.

Finally, students spoke passionately about the ways the course was a key to their professional identities. As one student noted, "I think it's difficult to consider oneself a 'professional' without an understanding of the legal issues that could potentially affect one's work, and I can't think of a professional librarian role for which there are not at least some significant legal implications to how one does one's work." Others offered similar observations, noting that the course "enabled me to be a better professional," that "I believe if we want to call our [graduate] program a professional program, then a class on the legal issues around our field is a must," and "if LIS programs claim to offer a comprehensive education that aligns with the values of the ALA, there can be no denying that legal issues coursework should be required."

ANALYSIS AND NEXT STEPS

These responses from former students align strongly with their initial end-of-semester evaluations. Whether they had just entered the job market, were completing a half-decade of work in their planned career, or had spent several years exploring a series of new jobs, or even new fields, students found the course useful and empowering. Speaking about the copyright materials in particular, one student summed up their feelings: "I think this was one of the best courses I took in grad school. It was incredibly helpful in learning more about copyright and other legal issues from a library perspective, which has enabled me to be a better professional. I still regularly utilize some of the knowledge and skills I learned in that class to provide guidance on copyright or enhance my understanding of other legal issues I encounter in my professional life."

Overall, this study suggests the potential for legal education in LIS programs to transform the library profession as a whole. By empowering students to understand and advocate for legal issues such as open access, intellectual freedom, and more equitable library policies, the course laid a foundation for systemic change. Students spoke passionately about the ways the course offered them "the footing and understanding of legal issues to make sure I protect my users and my library." Another student noted that no other courses offered anything comparable: "I look up and use the daily notes I took for this class at least once a semester. I don't do that for any other class I took in grad school." One student put a fine point on the gaps the course had filled and the potential it had unlocked:

> Honestly, this was the most valuable course I took during library school. I didn't get this information anywhere else during my time in library school—not in courses, internships, or student jobs. I am dealing with intellectual property issues fairly regularly in my job, and I truly don't think this sort of thing has ever occurred to anybody here before . . . Having an understanding of intellectual property issues has just really been invaluable as I try to improve our standards of professionalism and rein in the decisions of my predecessors.

Further study would be valuable to see if former students feel the same at the ten, fifteen, and twenty-year marks. If other LIS programs adopt some version of this course, as many former students recommended, those courses would also benefit from this type of analysis and evaluation. As one student noted, "I am frequently glad to have taken this class and wish that some of my colleagues at other locations had the basic knowledge I gained from this class." In addition to expanding this course offering to other LIS programs, the students' responses also suggest that more education which covers these topics should be made available for librarians at every stage of their careers. One former student spelled this out by writing, "I wish I could take this class again. It would be more valuable now that I have a professional context in which to apply its lessons."

An understanding of legal issues like copyright remains a significant gap for librarians at every stage of their careers. As scholars such as John Eye have noted, "Without adequate knowledge and awareness to be thoughtfully engaged, current frustration with intellectual property matters will continue to fester and distract from the efficiency and productivity of the academic environment."[6] This course suggests one approach for strengthening that knowledge base in order to improve service and empower librarians of every stripe to live up to the highest aspirations of the profession.

REFERENCES

American Library Association. (January 27, 2009). "ALA Core Competences of Librarianship." www.ala.org/educationcareers/sites/ala.org.educationcareers/ files/content/careers/corecomp/corecompetences/finalcorecompstat09.pdf.

Cariou v. Prince, 714 F.3d 694 (2d Cir. 2013).

Connaway, L. S., and R. R. Powell. (2010). *Basic Research Methods for Librarians*. Santa Barbara, CA: Libraries Unlimited.

Cross, W. M., and P. M. Edwards. (2011). "Preservice Legal Education for Academic Librarians within ALA-Accredited Degree Programs." *portal: Libraries and the Academy* 11, no. 1: 533–50.

Dames, K. M. (February 2006). "Library Schools and the Copyright Knowledge Gap." *Information Today* 23, no. 2: 1–15.

Dryden, J. (2011). "Learning about Law in Library School: A Snapshot." *Journal of Education for Library & Information Science* 52, no. 3: 184–97.

Eye, J. (2013). "Knowledge Level of Library Deans and Directors in Copyright Law." *Journal of Librarianship and Scholarly Communication* 2, no. 1: eP1103. http://dx.doi.org/10.7710/2162–3309.1103.

Kelly, K. (2018). "Feasibility Study on the Creation of a Virtual Center for Copyright Education for Professionals in Libraries, Archives, and Museums." Lyrasis. Available at https://copyright.columbia.edu/content/dam/copyright/Policy%20 Docs/Copyright%20Education%20Center%20Feasibility%20Study%20Report-1 –1.pdf.

Kerr, Orin S. (2007). "How to Read a Legal Opinion: A Guide for New Law Students." *Green Bag* 11, no. 51, 2nd series. Available at *SSRN*: https://ssrn.com/abstract =1160925.

McDermott, A. J. (2012). "Copyright: Regulation Out of Line with Our Digital Reality?" *Information Technology and Libraries* 31, no. 1: 7–20. http://dx.doi .org/10.6017/ital.v31i1.1859.

Miller, Nelson P., and Bradley J. Charles. (2009). "Meeting the Carnegie Report's Challenge to Make Legal Analysis Explicit—Subsidiary Skills to the IRAC Framework." *Journal of Legal Education* 59, no. 192.

Warner Bros. Entertainment, Inc. and J. K. Rowling v. RDR Books, 575 F.Supp.2d 513 (S.D.N.Y. 2008).

NOTES

1. American Library Association, 2009.
2. Kelly, 2018.
3. Cross and Edwards, 2011.
4. Miller and Charles, 2009; Kerr, 2007.
5. Connaway and Powell, 2010; Hank, Jordan, and Wildemuth, 2009.
6. Eye, 2013; McDermott, 2012.

About the Editors and Contributors

KEVIN L. SMITH is the dean of libraries at the University of Kansas. An attorney as well as a librarian, Smith was the director of copyright and scholarly communications at Duke University for ten years prior to moving to Kansas in 2016. He is a well-known writer and speaker on issues of copyright in higher education. Smith has been admitted to the bar in both Ohio and North Carolina.

ERIN L. ELLIS is the associate dean for research and learning services at Indiana University Bloomington Libraries. She holds an MLS degree from Emporia State University and a master's degree in higher education administration from the University of Kansas. Her research interests include organizational transformation, librarian instructor development, and information literacy. She has written and presented widely on these and other library-related topics. In addition, she is a consultant for organizational review and design.

JILL BECKER is the head of the Center for Undergraduate Initiatives and Engagement at the University of Kansas (KU) Libraries. Since 2012 she has worked to integrate information literacy and research skills into first-year experience programs and the undergraduate curriculum. Becker earned her bachelor's degree in English from KU, and her MLS degree from Emporia State University. At present, she is a doctoral candidate in higher education administration at KU. Her hopes as a librarian and teacher are to help undergraduate students gain a better understanding of the nature of information in today's world so that they can become informed seekers, users, and producers of information.

WILL CROSS is the director of the Copyright and Digital Scholarship Center at the North Carolina State University Libraries and an instructor at the University of North Carolina's School of Information and Library Science. Trained as a lawyer and librarian, he guides policy, speaks, and writes on legal frameworks that support open culture. As presenter coordinator for the ACRL's Scholarly Communication Roadshow, Cross has developed training materials and led workshops for international audiences from Ontario to Abu Dhabi. He currently serves as co-principal investigator on two IMLS-funded projects to develop copyright and scholarly communication training for librarians.

STEPHANIE DAVIS-KAHL is the collections and scholarly communications librarian and a professor at the Ames Library of Illinois Wesleyan University. She provides leadership for scholarly communication programs, including Digital Commons @ IWU, and serves as the managing faculty coeditor of the *Undergraduate Economic Review*. Her research interests focus on the intersections of scholarly communication and information literacy, particularly for undergraduates. In 2014, she was named a Mover & Shaker by *Library Journal* and was also awarded the ACRL Education and Behavioral Sciences Section's Distinguished Librarian Award.

ANA ENRIQUEZ is the scholarly communications outreach librarian at the Penn State University Libraries. Prior to that, she was a copyright specialist at the University of Michigan Library. She has also taught for CopyrightX, ACRL eLearning, Northeastern University, and Ithaca College. She is a graduate of Harvard College and the University of California-Berkeley School of Law.

ANNE T. GILLILAND is the scholarly communications officer at the University of North Carolina, Chapel Hill. She holds an MS degree in library and information science from the University of Tennessee and a JD from Capital University. Her legal knowledge supplements more than thirty years' experience working for and on behalf of academic libraries.

MERINDA KAYE HENSLEY is the digital scholarship liaison and instruction librarian and an associate professor at the University of Illinois at Urbana-Champaign. Her research investigates how the library can extend its information literacy mission into new areas, especially the librarian's pedagogical contribution and the factors that influence the decisions students make as creators of new knowledge. Hensley leads several library initiatives related to undergraduate research, including the publication of several undergraduate research journals, collecting undergraduate theses and capstone projects in the institutional repository, and administering the Image of Research competition.

CARLA MYERS is the coordinator of scholarly communications for the Miami University Libraries (Ohio). As part of her responsibilities, she provides information and guidance on copyright law, fair use, and authors' rights to members of the campus community. Her professional presentations and publications focus on copyright, open access, and affordable learning issues. She is also the cofounder and editor of the *Journal of Copyright in Education and Librarianship*. Myers holds a BA in psychology from the University of Akron and an MLIS degree from Kent State University.

ANALI MAUGHAN PERRY is the scholarly communication librarian at Arizona State University's ASU Library. In this role, she provides outreach and education to the ASU community regarding scholarly publishing and copyright, with particular emphasis on fair use, open access to scholarly information, and open education. She is currently a presenter for the ACRL's Scholarly Communication Roadshow.

LAURA QUILTER is the copyright and information policy librarian/attorney at the University of Massachusetts Amherst. She works with the UMass Amherst community on copyright and related matters, equipping faculty, students, and staff with the understanding they need to navigate copyright, fair use, open access, and related issues. Quilter is a frequent speaker who has taught and lectured to a wide variety of audiences. Her research interests are the intersection of copyright with intellectual freedom and access to knowledge, and more generally the public interest within technology and information law

KAREN SCHMIDT is the university librarian and university copyright officer at Illinois Wesleyan University, a position she has held since 2007. Prior to joining the IWU faculty, she served as associate university librarian for collections for many years at the University of Illinois at Urbana-Champaign. Schmidt is the editor of two books on library acquisitions and has published numerous articles on collection development, as well as librarian engagement in action research.

Index